evaluation of research

A SELECTION OF CURRENT PRACTICES

ORGANISATION FOR ECONOMIC CO-OPERATION AND DEVELOPMENT

Pursuant to article 1 of the Convention signed in Paris on 14th December, 1960, and which came into force on 30th September, 1961, the Organisation for Economic Co-operation and Development (OECD) shall promote policies designed:

- to achieve the highest sustainable economic growth and employment and a rising standard of living in Member countries, while maintaining financial stability, and thus to contribute to the development of the world economy;
- to contribute to sound economic expansion in Member as well as non-member countries in the process of economic development; and
- to contribute to the expansion of world trade on a multilateral, non-discriminatory basis in accordance with international obligations.

The original Member countries of the OECD are Austria, Belgium, Canada, Denmark, France, the Federal Republic of Germany, Greece, Iceland, Ireland, Italy, Luxembourg, the Netherlands, Norway, Portugal, Spain, Sweden, Switzerland, Turkey, the United Kingdom and the United States. The following countries acceded subsequently through accession at the dates hereafter: Japan (28th April, 1964), Finland (28th January, 1969), Australia (7th June, 1971) and New Zealand (29th May, 1973).

The Socialist Federal Republic of Yugoslavia takes part in some of the work of the OECD (agreement of 28th October, 1961).

Publié en français sous le titre:

ÉVALUATION
DE LA RECHERCHE

This report has been prepared by Mr. Michael Gibbons and Mr. Luke Georghiou under the direction of Mrs. Montserrat Solanes of the OECD Secretariat. The aim is not to present an exhaustive survey of evaluation practices in OECD countries, but rather to describe the main available techniques and the experience with their use in some interesting cases, the emphasis being mainly on university research.

It draws upon surveys of relevant practices in selected national institutions in the following countries: Canada, France, Germany, Japan, The Netherlands, Sweden, the United Kingdom and the United States. The findings of these surveys were extensively discussed, under the aegis of the OECD Committee for Scientific and Technological Policy, by its *Ad Hoc* Group on Scientific and University Research.

A large number of government and university officials have participated in the various stages of enquiries and discussions. The experts who carried out the country surveys should be specially thanked, notably Mrs. Heidi Kuusi for the surveys of France and Germany, Mr. Stewart Blume for the survey of The Netherlands, and Messrs. Michael Gibbons and Luke Georghiou for the surveys of the United Kingdom, the United States and Canada.

Lastly, special acknowledgement should be made of the valuable comments received from the *Ad Hoc* Group on Scientific and University Research, as well as of the help provided by interested countries for the preparation of the surveys.

This report was reviewed by the Committee for Scientific and Technological Policy, which recommended that it be made available to the public on the responsibility of the Secretary-General of OECD, who subsequently agreed.

Also available

SCIENCE, TECHNOLOGY, INDUSTRY REVIEW No. 1/Autumn 1986 (December 1986)

(90 86 01 1) ISBN 92-64-12888-3   129 pages £8.00   US$16.00   F80.00   DM35.00

Subscription (No. 2/Spring and No. 3/Autumn 1987)

ISSN 1010-5239 £15.00   US$30.00   F150.00   DM66.00

RECOMBINANT DNA SAFETY CONSIDERATIONS (September 1986)

(93 86 02 1) ISBN 92-64-12857-3   70 pages £6.00   US$12.00   F60.00   DM27.00

REVIEW OF NATIONAL SCIENCE AND TECHNOLOGY POLICY:

.   **FINLAND (March 1987)**

(92 87 02 1) ISBN 92-64-12928-6   154 pages £9.50   US$19.00   F95.00   DM42.00

.   **AUSTRALIA (August 1986)**

(92 86 05 1) ISBN 92-64-12851-4   120 pages £7.50   US$15.00   F75.00   DM33.00

INNOVATION POLICY:

.   **FRANCE (February 1987)**

(92 86 06 1) ISBN 92-64-12884-0   296 pages £16.00   US$32.00   F160.00   DM71.00

.   **IRELAND (March 1987)**

(92 87 01 1) ISBN 92-64-12918-9   76 pages £5.00   US$10.00   F50.00   DM22.00

INDUSTRY AND UNIVERSITY. New Forms of Co-operation and Communication (October 1984)

(92 84 04 1) ISBN 92-64-12607-4   70 pages £3.50   US$7.00   F35.00   DM16.00

SCIENCE AND TECHNOLOGY POLLICY OUTLOOK – 1985 (June 1985)

(92 85 03 1) ISBN 92-64-12738-0   90 pages £5.50   US$11.00   F55.00   DM24.00

CONTENTS

FOREWORD

Evaluation of research is a general concern of OECD Member countries. It is carried out in both public and private sector organisations at all levels – from that of determining individual performance to that aimed at determining the quality and effectiveness of research programmes or the scientific standing and performance of whole institutions. Nevertheless, the evaluation procedures employed in the public sector are often very different from those practised by private firms owing to the different nature of the latter's objectives.

The recent increase in interest shown in the evaluation of research can be explained by several factors including slow (sometimes zero) growth research budgets, increased supranational programming, the growing importance of R&D for all economic activities and, lastly, the consequent need to lay down priorities whatever the area of research (fundamental, applied, development).

The present report is primarily intended to inform people interested in the practices used in different countries. Its deliberately technical approach will help both scientists and decision-makers unfamiliar with these procedures to define the most relevant practices in the light of analysis of the advantages and limitations of them.

The main emphasis is on university research. The section on the methodological aspects of evaluation therefore endeavours particularly to describe procedures based in one way or another on peer review. However, the priority given by the authors to certain university-type procedures in no way excludes other management practices of different institutions with R&D activities.

As the authors point out several times in the report, the elements of evaluation are: scope, purpose, criteria and organisation. The study of the practices currently used cannot, therefore, be expected to produce universal standard procedures. It is important at this point to warn against the risk of confusing significant concepts such as what we shall call the *evaluation approach (or protocol)*, for which a number of general rules can be given, with the *method of evaluation* (for example, peer review) and *procedures* (surveys, visits), which themselves call for different kinds of *tools* (questionnaires, data banks, etc.).

The framework for evaluation in OECD countries reflects their various political and administrative cultures and varies from a pluralistic, decentralised approach to centralised co-ordinated systems placing legally defined frameworks for evaluation across the public sector.

Evaluation incurs costs directly and indirectly, through the opportunity cost of the time of those involved in peer review and the cost to those being evaluated in terms of time and disruption. Direct costs vary but they usually represent less than one per cent of the programme budget. The cost of an evaluation should be proportionate to the scale, importance and innovativeness of a programme.

Future work should continue to collect data on national experiences with evaluations and extend the work to consider the implications for the social sciences and humanities which are becoming more and more important and where there is widespread concern that techniques developed for the natural sciences may be uncritically transferred. It should also look more closely at the evaluation practices in those areas where quality of research is only one of the objectives to be obtained. Evaluation should also address the structures that are supposed to deliver scientific knowledge for the careful analysis of the effects of evaluation on subsequent research performance.

SUMMARY

Evaluation of research is an increasing activity within the OECD Member countries. It is carried out in both public and private sector organisations at all levels from that of determining individual performance to that aimed at determining the quality and effectiveness of research programmes or the scientific standing and performance of whole institutions.

Elements in the organisation of evaluation

The *scope* of an evaluation includes the types of research involved, the object or level to be evaluated and the time frame within which it is to be carried out (*ex-ante, interim* or *ex-post*). It may be problematic defining the boundaries of the type and level of research involved.

It is very important to be explicit about the *purpose* for undertaking an evaluation and this should be established in a framework of co-operation between the users of the evaluation, those carrying out the evaluation and those being evaluated.

Criteria for evaluation reflect the type of research and range from scientific excellence to economic and social benefit. Most research involves a combination of these objectives and hence criteria. For project selection the criteria generally applied are scientific merit, the appropriateness of the finance sought and criteria designed to ensure that programme objectives are being met. Evaluation of industrial relevance is problematic. In *ex-post* evaluation, criteria may be extended beyond the original objectives and may involve comparisons, possibly with alternative ways of meeting the objectives.

In the *organisation* of an evaluation the choice of evaluators is crucial. Member countries have various ways of assembling groups of expertise whose impartiality will withstand close professional scrutiny. For smaller countries in particular, the inclusion of foreign experts is often adopted. When it is desirable to broaden the evaluation team to include industrialists, civil servants or even lay people there is a double problem of getting the balance right for the task in hand and providing non-experts with appropriate information so that they can contribute effectively to the evaluation process. Even when trying to relate the results of research to broader socio-economic goals, teams often give more attention to the substantive aspects of the research being undertaken rather than whether if fulfils the higher order objectives.

Clear guidelines should be given to the evaluation team which include the procedures to be followed throughout the study and define the scope, purpose and criteria to be applied. The evaluation team needs to be aware of the context in which the final results are likely to be used. Lack of clarity about the boundaries of an evaluation may threaten the basis of collaboration upon which the whole exercise rests.

Methods and techniques

The methods and techniques used should be appropriate to the evaluation and not determine its structure. Methods should not be adopted simply because they may be applied or easily adapted to existing data bases. Currently, the predominant method employed in the evaluation of research is based on achieving a consensus of expert judgements. This is the case whether the evaluation is trying to establish the quality of research activity or to determine economic implications of a new technology. The most widely used approach is the peer review process. Some criticism of its limitations has led to various experimental modifications. In this study three types of peer review are identified:

i) *Direct peer review* defined as a review by a scientific peer (or peers) carried out specifically for the purpose of determining, and confined to, questions of scientific merit. Criticisms of the method arise when it is applied across specialities especially when resources are severely constrained;

ii) *Modified peer review* is similar but the criteria are broadened to include socio-economic considerations. Balanced judgements are necessary in these circumstances;

iii) *Indirect peer review* adds information based upon peer evaluation made for different purposes and at different times. The majority of this information and analysis is bibliometric.

Bibliometrics is founded upon the assumptions that the output of scientific research is consistently represented by articles appearing in scientific journals; that the number of citations to these articles is a legitimate indicator of their impact or quality; and that accurate data is available. A review of the strengths and weaknesses of the various techniques is given in the main text. Some problems with bibliometrics include the time taken for analysis, bias towards English language journals, poor coverage in the data base of certain fields and lack of adequate coverage of technology.

Process evaluations address the structures and mechanisms of research and are at their most useful where the research has a complex or innovative structure or where several interfaces are involved such as those that might exist between universities or government laboratories and industry.

A significant proportion of scientific research is justified in terms of the socio-economic benefits expected to arise as a result of it. However, linkages between R&D and socio-economic impact are subtle and complex. Consequently, experience with models which try to correlate R&D investment with a variety of economic output measures has been mixed. Such impact analyses are rarely used. The approach most often adopted is to seek the views of the users of the research where these can be identified. The case study approach remains widely applied but can be time consuming, expensive and presents problems of generalisation. Technological indicators are gaining ground as policy tools but their scope goes beyond R&D to the innovation process.

Administration of evaluation

The framework for evaluation in OECD countries reflects their political and administrative cultures and varies from a pluralistic, decentralised approach to centralised co-ordinated systems placing legally defined frameworks for evaluation across the public sector.

Choice of evaluators for the peer review system is typically carried out by existing committees or their secretariats. It is important that evaluators are seen to be objective and hence also the process by which they are selected. The inclusion of foreign experts provides such a mechanism but is restricted by lack of knowledge of a country and its language. Professional evaluators may be sited within an organisation or engaged under contract. The advantage of having evaluators within an organisation is the relevant knowledge they may accumulate and development of an interface with decision-makers. Independent evaluators may draw upon a varied experience and unbiased view but can lack familiarity with the subject matter. Professional ethics for evaluators are important.

Evaluation incurs costs directly and indirectly, through the opportunity cost of the time of those involved in peer review and the cost for those being evaluated in terms of time and disruption. Direct costs vary but a common target figure is one per cent of the programme budget. The cost of an evaluation should be proportionate to the scale, importance and innovativeness of a programme.

Evaluation of scientific research in universities

Evaluation is taking place throughout the university system in most Member countries at a multiplicity of levels. There is a tension between mutual evaluations by scientific peers, which are used to shape the direction and maintain the quality of various disciplines, and the wider demands made upon evaluation as an instrument for changing structures, for determining the allocation of resources and for assessing the performance of certain scientific areas in relation to national needs. Much effort has been focused upon demonstrating quality of science to a wider audience which may not be fully convinced by the peer review system.

Only in isolated examples are indicators used in a mechanical sense for the allocation of resources but where difficult decisions have to be made their consideration is becoming more common despite misgivings. Allocation systems work best where a clear response to a well defined proposal is required. Where whole areas of science or institutions are under appraisal the process is more political. *Ex-post* evaluations when initiated internally are generally aimed at improving performance by self-scrutiny. In other cases evaluations were intended to satisfy a government requirement that the objectives, implementation and outcome of research expenditure be examined.

Evaluation of mission-oriented research

Mission-oriented research is interpreted as including three institutional forms:
- Research council programmes with industrial objectives;
- Extramural research sponsored by government mission agencies; and
- Intramural research sponsored by government mission agencies.

The evaluation of mission-oriented research should be relatively straightforward but this is rarely the case. Objectives often have yet to be fully achieved and both time delays and the complex links to products make *ex-post* evaluation difficult. Both university and agency sponsored programmes have concentrated in their evaluations on the more attainable goal of user satisfaction. Clients may be internal to the organisation or, in the case of strategic research, numerous but difficult to identify. Potential clients may often find it difficult to place a value on the research for they are unable themselves to answer questions about long term developments.

Many countries are currently reviewing the appropriate role and scale of government sponsored research and a recurrent request for evaluators has been to try to compare intramural and extramural research. Most commonly the criterion of comparison has been that of quality of research, with government laboratories sensitive to the suggestion that they do not perform research of comparable quality to that in universities.

International programmes

International programmes may proceed in a number of forms including bilateral contact, multilateral programmes and programmes involving assistance to developing countries. All place additional demands and criteria upon evaluation including logistic problems. Issues include what research is appropriate for a collaborative rather than national approach and how the benefits of collaboration may be secured. For developing countries, many techniques developed in industrial economies are not easily transferable.

Conclusions

There are currently no techniques available which allow different specialities to be compared and ranked through committees responsible for funding research carrying out these activities. Certain bibliometric techniques allow the identification of emerging new fields and an alternative form of ranking is by age of specialities. However, the techniques are more likely to identify promising individuals than promising areas and in this respect will reinforce the existing peer review process.

There are many experiments seeking to enhance peer review by introducing a broader base of information. Though bibliometric methods are diffusing into the peer review process, this has been slow and in no case have we found substantial support for the idea that it will eventually replace peer review. More significant is the growing use of social science methods, questionnaires and structured interviews, to gather information. These can reach large numbers of practising scientists and with the development of electronic communication networks may directly challenge the authority of peer review panels.

The question of value for money from investments in scientific research is increasingly asked in *ex-post* evaluations. In both the elaboration of methods of evaluation and in the experiences of evaluation practices of Member countries the development of value for money criteria lags considerably behind criteria for scientific quality. Much research is needed here.

There is insufficient communication between the results of *ex-post* evaluations and subsequent *ex-ante* resource allocation decisions. *Ex-ante* evaluations are still largely the preserve of expert consensus while *ex-post* evaluations are increasingly becoming the preserve of a cadre of professional evaluators. Care must be taken to avoid a separation between the two.

Future work should continue to collect data on national experiences with evaluations and extend the work to consider the implications for the social sciences and humanities where there is widespread concern that techniques developed for the natural sciences may be incritically transferred. It should also look more closely at the evaluation practices in those areas where quality of research is only one of the objectives to be obtained. Evaluation should also address the structures that are supposed to deliver scientific knowledge for the careful analysis of the effects of evaluation on subsequent research performance.

I. INTRODUCTION

Evaluation of research is carried out in both public and private sector organisations, at all levels, in every OECD Member country. In some of these countries, evaluation is more systematically pursued than in others but this should not obscure the fact that evaluation – trying to determine whether policies have really made any difference – is, and probably always has been very widespread. In this study, we have examined only a small subset of the total activity of evaluation; that concerned with the evaluation of research. But, even here, we have encountered an upsurge of interest and, in some cases activity. However, research covers many different types of activity and because of this the evaluation of research is undertaken for many reasons and in a variety of contexts. One consequence of this is that evaluations differ greatly in their scope, purpose, criteria employed and, to a somewhat lesser extent, their methods. This diversity has made it extremely difficult to compress our findings into a completely satisfactory conceptual framework or to elicit from the empirical materials a code of practice to guide policy-makers in the future. Indeed, the analysis of the evaluation of research in a given country depends on the specific social function of science in that country, and in particular on the structure and organisation of the national research system. In practical terms, this means that the problem of evaluation will not be perceived and, therefore, not be approached in the same way in different countries and that not much progress will be made by a culling of experiences of other countries in search of one unique "best technique". In evaluation studies as in every other area of research the method has to be appropriate to the aims and purposes of the evaluation. In the most effective of the evaluations we have encountered the purpose, scope and criteria to be applied have been thoroughly worked out and discussed both by the institution requesting the evaluation and by those being evaluated.

1. Why evaluation?

The evaluation of research is currently a preoccupation of every Member country; at the very least expressions of interest in the topic appear to be virtually universal. Why should this be so? In particular, why should this be so in the mid-1980s? The most frequent answer is given in terms of the "realities of economic life". Beginning with the oil crises of 1973 and 1974 and throughout the recession that followed them, economic activity slowed down while inflation and unemployment increased. For most government research agencies as well as for the universities, this recession has implied a period of austerity and a critical review of patterns of expenditure. As far as scientific research, particularly that carried out in the universities, was concerned, budget growth rates diminished and in some cases became negative in real terms. In an environment of declining resources, so the argument runs, new activities can be initiated only at the expense of existing ones because all research has to be carried out within a preset envelope of expenditure. In this situation it is necessary to identify which current activities are worth keeping and which are to be cut back in order to allow new things to emerge. The identification and preservation of "worth" is one of the principal aims of evaluation.

No-one will want to deny that the Member countries have had to weather the storm of a deep recession in economic activity, nor that such depressions make difficult choices necessary. But, science as an institution has existed long enough for it to have endured many recessions and in no case have these caused an upsurge of interest in evaluating the results of research; cutbacks have come and gone but few have questioned the quality of research currently being carried out. Why, in the 1980s, then has the evaluation of research become a focus for so much activity? If the explanation is not entirely economic, is it then merely a reaction to an uncertain future? While the evaluation of individual performance has always been intrinsic to science, our experience in carrying out this study does seem to indicate that there is a novel element involved in the sense that in addition to this type of evaluation the performance of research institutions, research councils, governmental laboratories, and universities are also being scrutinised. The emergence of new, exploratory types of evaluation at the institutional level has generated uncertainty, not to say deep insecurity, among those responsible for managing research. At each level of social organisation, it seems, there is a fear that a technique of evaluation will be found that shows their activities in a less than favourable light. One consequence of this has been a good deal of what might be called "defensive" evaluation; that is, rather tentative one-off evaluation of projects and programmes, etc., where it is not clear what the purpose of the evaluation is to achieve or how it might affect the way things are currently done.

2. Growth, competition and new technologies

There is, we feel, a deeper problem of this than simply falling budgets or the paranoia of those being evaluated. It is the *growth* of science and research related activities themselves that is the origin of the resource problems, not the most recent economic recession. During the past 50 years or so, most OECD countries have witnessed an explosion of scientific and technological activities in both the public and private sectors. The point we would make is that science, if it is to remain healthy depends upon competition between experts and that as science has grown competition has intensified for intellectual leadership of each field or sub-speciality. So the question of what is the best science would arise naturally from the dynamics of science itself. It is part and parcel of the activities of specialists to try to differentiate their activities from one another but in so doing they also indicate where pathways of future development are likely to lie. The change that has taken place during the past 25 years in most OECD countries is that competition for intellectual leadership (and, therefore, resources) in research of all types has been moved from the individual to the institutional level. It is arguable that the intensification of the spirit of competition within science would have emerged without either the oil crises or the subsequent recessions. In this case, as in so many others, the depression has merely brought to light, sooner rather than later perhaps, certain structural features of our socio-economic life. Competition is an intrinsic part of the institutional life of contemporary science, and growth in the interest in evaluating the quality of output of research is an important element in the orchestration of that enterprise. Perhaps the most important novel element in the 1980s is the growing awareness that increasing competitiveness and evaluation are but two sides of the same coin.

A second factor, perhaps also promoted by the recession, but which on its own has served to promote growth in interest in the evaluation of research arises from the technological side.

14

Industry itself appears to be caught in a wave of technological innovations. Many economists have argued that the developed world is currently going through a major transformation of its industrial structure; that the thrust of this transformation is technological; and that it is manifested in the application of the new technologies of robotics, computers, telecommunications, etc., to the ways in which goods and services are produced and distributed. These new technologies are widely believed to be particularly open in their development to new ideas and methods arising from within science itself. But, which sciences, which disciplines, which experts are the most likely to provide new technologies with the fuel for their longer term development? Here, evaluations of economic potential of "exploitable areas of science" is necessary but whatever success is achieved in this area, the impetus to evaluation has less to do with the overall financial situation than with securing a niche in the next phase of industrial expansion.

The thrust of these observations is that the way in which a country will be able to deal with its problems of structural change will depend both upon the stage of development its scientific and technological institutions have reached as well as the political and industrial culture within which the economy is situated. An awareness of national individuality in this respect has guided this investigation of research evaluation. The study which was carried out in 1984 and 1985 included Canada, France, Japan, West Germany, the Netherlands, Sweden, the United Kingdom and the United States. While reports on these countries have provided a major input other sources, notably the OECD workshop on science and technology indicators in the higher education sector[1] have been especially beneficial as has information from other Member countries and the EEC. We have also made extensive use of the now considerable literature on evaluation particularly in that part of the report concerned with current thinking and practice with regard to methodological issues (see especially Chapter 3).

It is appropriate here to mention the limitations of this study in what is a very large subject area. Apart from the limited number of countries covered, it is important to stress that a comprehensive survey was not carried out of the full range of organisations and practices involved in the evaluation of R&D. What was sought was in particular evidence as to how evaluation was interacting with the university system (and this meant to a large extent the peer review system of *ex-ante* evaluation) and more generally a selection of evaluation activities in other government agencies which highlighted the culture and practice of evaluation in that country. The object of this report, then, is not to provide a handbook for evaluators in the sense of a prescriptive guide or a directory. Even if the data had been available, differences in administrative cultures would have made this an exercise of dubious value. Rather, the intention is to provide a perspective on the activity of evaluation and by discussing a selection of experiences of Member countries to discern the directions which are emerging in this activity.

3. Structure of the report

The results of our inquiries into the current state of the art in the evaluation of research are presented in eight main chapters. After a brief introduction, Chapter 2 is concerned with the scope and purpose of evaluations and how the choice of these affect the criteria for evaluations. A brief description of the main types of criteria currently employed is given. In Chapter 3, some of the principal methodologies and techniques being used currently in various types of evaluation are reviewed. Here, we have tried to organise the range of options available to evaluators in terms of the situations in which they have been used. The principal distinction drawn is primarily between the various types of peer review and other approaches. The next four Chapters aim to summarise the experiences of Member countries as encountered during this study. In Chapter 4 we set out some brief descriptions of the experiences of several countries in the organisation of evaluation, and we also discuss some aspects of the legal framework and the costs of evaluation. Chapter 5 is devoted to an exploration of evaluation as it occurs currently in the context of scientific research in universities and similar institutions. In this Chapter we devote considerable attention to the establishment of priorities, to evaluation at the project level, and to the effect on *ex-post* evaluation of the organisational level at which the evaluation is carried out. Chapter 6 is devoted to evaluation of mission-oriented research carried out in a variety of contexts. Chapter 7 describes some experiences of evaluation of international programmes and Chapter 8 consists of some concluding remarks.

II. ELEMENTS IN THE ORGANISATION OF EVALUATION

Before moving to a discussion of the methods and techniques being used in evaluations of research and the experiences of Member countries in applying them, it is necessary to consider four elements that are present in every evaluation and which comprise the context in which the evaluation will be carried out. These elements are: scope, purpose, criteria and organisation. It is the experience of each Member country involved in evaluating research that each of these four elements must be clearly articulated beforehand if the evaluators as well as those being evaluated are to communicate effectively. This is important because, as we shall see, the techniques available for evaluating research all depend in one way or another on the participation of those involved in the research process. Clearly, the elements listed above are interrelated. For example, the scope and purpose of an evaluation will largely determine the criteria to be applied and the form of organisation best suited to carry out the evaluations. In an effective evaluation, the four elements will be mutually adjusted and the precondition of this is a clear statement of each.

A. SCOPE OF EVALUATION

1. Type of research

The scope of an evaluation comprises a number of different things, notably the types of research involved, the level of the evaluation and the time span on which the evaluation will focus. With regard to the first, the scope of evaluation must specify whether the research in question is basic, applied, strategic or product-oriented. The difficulty in classifying research is well known but for the purposes of the present study mission-oriented research is treated separately.

In the execution of an evaluative study, the criteria applied and the methods used differ with the type of research being examined. In some ways, this is unfortunate because not every evaluation will encompass one type of research only. More often, in fact, the various types of research will be blended in various projects, programmes, institutions and if these are subject to evaluation then it should be structured to take into account the different types of research involved. For example, the blending of different types of research occurs frequently in the evaluation of medical research where not only is there a recurrent tension between basic and applied (clinical) research but also between both types of research and the goals set for medical research institutions by the relevant government departments. In these cases, defining the scope of the evaluation is not straightforward and, although it is easy enough to divide the study into different parts which reflect the primary types of research being considered, the original problem returns when it comes to combining the elements into an overall assessment.

2.   Object of evaluation

Perhaps the most important aspect in determining the scope of a particular evaluation lies in determining the object to be evaluated. Is it to be the individual researchers, or the research group? Is it to be project-centred or to comprise whole disciplines or fields of science or technological research; or on complex programmes spread across many institutions; or on the international aspect of collaborative research programmes? In fact, evaluations can, and do, take place on each of these levels though among the OECD Member countries a larger number of evaluations take place at the level of individual researchers or individual projects where the process is firmly institutionalised rather than at the highest levels where national scientific capabilities would come under scrutiny.

There is, however, a real problem in dealing with this aspect of the scope of an evaluation and it arises because the level in the research system at which it is desired to carry out the evaluation cannot always be easily isolated from the layers both above and below it. Unless every evaluation is to be fully comprehensive, methods need to be elaborated to define the unit of analysis which express clearly the boundaries of the evaluation. These boundaries, as we shall see, become very important when it becomes necessary to explain the purpose of a particular evaluation.

3.   Time frame

A third aspect of the scope of evaluation concerns the time frame within which it is to be carried out. Three dimensions of this may be distinguished; the evaluations that are *ex-ante*, *ex-post* and *interim*.

Ex-ante evaluation is closely associated with the formulation and execution of policy for research. Nevertheless, according to the level to which it applies (government, institution, laboratory), the function and significance of evaluation will not be the same. This may explain the apparent paradox of the major importance of *ex-ante* evaluation for the establishment of research priorities, whereas for the universities this type of evaluation loses its significance since it follows a prior budget decision in any case. It may perhaps be regretted that *ex-ante* evaluation is not practised more in the universities at the same time as budgeting and programming.

For many observers, *interim evaluation* is indistinguishable from current management or accounting operations. In fact, programmes are usually in stages followed by a progress report. The main interest of *interim* evaluation lies in the fact that it interacts with programming and can therefore be a management tool for the decision-makers. *Ex-post evaluation* comprises an assessment of the results obtained and an analysis of the way in which the resources and means allocated to a programme have been used as compared with the initial and any additional objectives. It queries the budgeting procedures used and is forward looking in this sense since its results are included in future programming. *Ex-post* evaluation cannot be the same at the different government, institution or laboratory levels. There is thus a whole series of types of *ex-post* evaluation. It should also be noted that the end of a scientific programme is not necessarily followed by an *ex-post* evaluation. When this does take place, it is usually requested by the institution itself with a view to the future, for example when considering a new direction for its activities.

It is thus more than an evaluation and may well take place long after completion of the programme. In fact, the greater the programme's socio-economic implications, the longer the interval is likely to be.

Ideally, in any research system there should be a feedback loop connecting a given *ex-post* evaluation with the next phase of *ex-ante* evaluations, but it seems to be the case empirically that *ex-ante* evaluations are regular and direct and systematic while *ex-post* evaluations are often *ad hoc. Interim* evaluations – evaluations that take place during the course of a project or programme – are numerically small and in most cases are indistinguishable from monitoring the progress of prior allocation decisions. As Figure 1 illustrates, if programmes run in close succession, the *ex-ante* evaluation of the second programme can only benefit from the results of the first part of the *interim* evaluation of the first. The *ex-post* evaluation of the first programme is only available to the *ex-ante* evaluation of the next programme but one. Because *ex-ante* and *ex-post* evaluation are carried out at opposite ends, so to speak, of the decision-making process they clearly fill different functions; functions which are related to the purpose of the evaluation. To discussion of this we now turn.

Figure 1

Chronology of evaluation

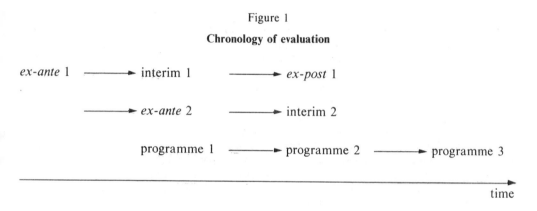

B. PURPOSE OF EVALUATION

As has already been indicated, evaluations take place at a variety of levels from that of the individual researcher to that of the most comprehensive assessment of national research capability. Further, it is necessary to recognise as a concomitant of the social organisation of research, that there is a hierarchy of objectives for any particular evaluation. For example procedures governing academic appointments constitute a simple evaluation process; typically, a committee tries to evaluate the past research performance and future potential of a candidate. But, on the level of the institution (i.e. the university) an evaluation could be concerned with the appointment committee's procedures and not with candidates; and an evaluation of committee procedures might call into question the operation of the national peer review system, which might in turn reflect upon the procedures by which scientists are nominated to learned societies, etc. In other words, the question of the purpose of a particular evaluation is easier to pose than it is to answer. Yet, in the experience gained carrying out this study, there would appear to be no more important factor determining the success of an evaluation than that its purpose (or purposes) be made clear at the outset. Evaluation studies relate to the research system in so many ways that it is so difficult to distinguish what is internal to the system being evaluated from what is external. The boundary dividing internal from external is a movable one and it moves not only with the level of organisation being considered as might be expected but also with the type of question being asked.

It is, thus, extremely important to be explicit about the purposes for undertaking an evaluation and this is perhaps best worked out in a dialogue between those who want the evaluation and those who are going to be evaluated. It makes a great deal of difference to the degree of collaboration from those being evaluated if the results of the study are to be used to select areas of research for future development, or to reorient existing allocations or simply as a means of cutting off existing resources. At the level of the individual or research team it is important to know whether the study is being carried out in the context of encouragement and support or whether the results will be used in subsequent decision-making. The former may generate a climate of collaboration, but uncertainty about the latter will most likely breed a suspicion that divides the community and may render the evaluation ineffective.

1. *Ex-ante* evaluation

The purpose of evaluation is also difficult to separate from scope particularly in relation to the level and timing of evaluation. *Ex-ante evaluation is closely associated with the formulation and execution of policy for research*. At the highest level it is concerned with the allocation of resources for scientific activity as a whole, though in many countries this may be a disaggregated process operating at the level below, where priorities are established. Here, the choice is between areas of science and historical precedent is usually strong; choice being made mainly at the margin in terms of areas in which to make initiatives and, more rarely, which areas to run down. Of course, decisions of this type have a political aspect and, while criteria such as potential return on investment or the scientific promise of the area are implicitly used, factors such as the effectiveness of a particular lobby or the need to compete with the performance of another country are often important considerations. Higher level evaluations also form a part of the planning process for science and may address such issues as manpower requirements or the need for major facilities. The third level is concerned with the allocation of resources to individual programmes and projects. When this is carried out by peer review methods it is performed by the scientific community itself, but as wider criteria are brought to bear, the decision-making process itself may be modified (see Chapter 3).

2. *Ex-post* evaluation

Ex-post evaluations may be carried out for several reasons. They may form an integral part of *ex-ante* allocation decisions in the sense that the past performance of the institution or research of concern forms an important input to subsequent decisions. Where *ex-post* evaluations are commissioned specifically, their purpose will depend on the user of the evaluations. Evaluation can be an instrument of accountability and hence be used by the body to which the project, programme or institution is accountable in order to ascertain whether it has fulfilled or is fulfilling its prescribed function. In this case the aim is often to determine the standing of the project or the body being evaluated in relation to the state of the art nationally or internationally. For programmes which are ongoing, the purpose of the evaluation is likely to be also to improve its effectiveness.

The initiative for evaluations does not always come from the organisation to which those carrying out the research are accountable; research managers may also commission it themselves. To some extent this is normal internal management practice but where an outside organisation is brought in to perform the evaluation there are broader requirements. In part, evaluation will be intended to legitimate the research to an external audience, be it scientific or political. Benefits through suggestions for improved performance are, of course, also sought.

Thus, at one end of the spectrum, a university department might operate a visiting external review process to reassure itself and its peers that its academic standards are being maintained, while at the macro-level a science funding agency may wish to demonstrate the worth of science to a very broad political audience.

C. CRITERIA FOR EVALUATION

Among the researchers and policy-makers in the Member countries there is widespread agreement that criteria for evaluation must be related to the scope and purpose of the evaluation: to the former because scope embraces the type of research to be evaluated as well as the organisational level at which the evaluation will be carried out; to the latter because purpose will indicate the use that is to be made of the results of the evaluation. Thus, there will be little argument that different criteria will be needed depending on whether, say, scientific quality or value for money is the main issue. Criteria should also reflect the requirements of the user, most frequently the organisation funding the research, as well as the level of aggregation at which the evaluation has to be executed.

As a starting point consider the spectrum of types of research ranging from basic research through applied to product-oriented developments. In terms of criteria, there is a similar parallel spectrum running from criteria for identifying quality in research to criteria for identifying value for money. In universities or other institutions where basic research is carried out, criteria for evaluation may be expected to elaborate various dimensions of scientific excellence, while in mission-oriented agencies or in industry, criteria related to economic and social goals will tend to be more in evidence. The former may be expected to reflect the various indicators of excellence articulated by the scientific community itself while the latter will reflect the economic rewards that accrue to those firms that successfully compete in the market place. Between these two extremes lie the vast majority of research activities which are neither entirely basic research nor entirely product development; which are neither entirely in the universities nor entirely in the market place; where neither the operation of the peer review system nor the market mechanism is the appropriate criterion for evaluation. In most OECD Member countries, there is a general trend towards developing criteria that are applicable to this vast middle ground and it is being approached from both ends of the spectrum. For example, we see attempts being made by universities and research councils in a number of countries to broaden the peer review system while industry itself is beginning to experiment with the idea of strategic research as a way of coping with the technical demands of the innovation process.

1. Criteria for project selection

Still, it is not always easy to translate these trends into specific, distinct criteria for evaluation. Probably the most frequently articulated criteria are those which govern project selection in research funding agencies. Each country has developed its own particular statement of these as essentially *ex-ante* assessments of scientific quality but in content they are remarkably similar. In these guidelines, the first criterion to be addressed is usually that of scientific merit. This may have several dimensions, including:

a) The competence of the researcher to perform the proposed work;
b) The significance of the proposed work for its speciality; which may include as sub-criteria such issues as timeliness and promise of the research, etc.; and
c) The effects of the work on other areas of science.

21

With regard to the first dimension, systems vary in the relative weight they place upon researchers compared with the proposed research. At one limit is the system in which the holding of an academic post is itself sufficient for a researcher to obtain funds while at the other limit is an assessment system where work is judged without the names of those submitted to it being revealed. At the core of the second dimension of scientific merit is peer judgement of the contribution that the research will make to its field. Under this assessment issues such as the originality of the work, the use its results will be to other researchers in the field and the scientific feasibility of the work are addressed. The third dimension, the effect of the work on other areas of science, what sometimes has been termed external criteria, looks at the broader scientific significance of the research. In this regard, the United States National Science Foundation has articulated a related criterion for selection: the effect of the work on the infrastructure of science and engineering.

The second set of criteria to be found explicitly or implicitly in most systems concerns the level of funds required. It is necessary for researchers to convince those sitting in judgement that the resources requested are commensurate with the specified research task. A more complex aspect of this is to determine whether public funds are necessary for the work to proceed. Clearly, this is a more frequently used criterion when funding for industry is involved because universities are less likely to have significant resources of their own for research. Known as the additionality (or incrementality) criterion, it is always problematic to apply because it deals with the hypothetical situation and one in which those applying for funds have a vested interest in giving a positive answer.

A third set of criteria consists of a group designed to ensure that the specific objectives of a particular programme are being met. Normally, these would concern the relation of the research to some social or economic goal but other more specific criteria such as a requirement to collaborate with other universities or industry or to link with other projects in a programme are also used. The criterion of industrial relevance is frequently a consideration here, but in this case it may be applied in a variety of ways ranging from a judgement by a panel to a mandatory requirement for matching funding. Even this seemingly objective criterion may be difficult to apply because in some circumstances placing a value on contributions made in *kind* is often difficult to assess quantitatively.

The idea that the potential utility of research should be established is clearly strongest in mission-oriented research but in recent years this criterion has become an important consideration for longer term research falling in the strategic category. The obvious difficulty in applying strategic criteria is the uncertainty involved, not only in terms of whether the research itself will succeed in technological terms but also whether the goal itself will turn out in the end to have market or other social relevance. Strategic research is clearly an area in which continuous evaluation is required.

2. Criteria for *ex-post* evaluation

The criteria for *ex-post* evaluation are, as one might expect, not fundamentally different from those in operation at the *ex-ante* stage. Typically, however, they are enacted at a higher level of aggregation because *ex-post* assessments of individual projects, unless built into the following selection stage or as part of a sample, is generally considered not to be very cost effective. As a consequence, the focus in *ex-post* evaluations is usually at the programme or institutional level. At these levels the criterion of scientific merit remains important but it is difficult to apply because the collective worth of a range of individual projects is difficult to aggregate.

The economic and social impact of a programme, as remarked above, may extend beyond the original objectives. The objectives of the sponsor may also have changed during the course of the programme and may now demand criteria for evaluation different from those used in the original selection. For example, economic relevance may have increased in its weighting if a commercial opportunity has appeared; on the other hand, if commercial interest has receded, even relatively applied programmes may find themselves being assessed against newly perceived basic science options. Also brought into consideration in *ex-post* evaluation is the criterion of efficiency. This criterion bears on whether the programme could have been undertaken earlier or with fewer resources or with less bureaucracy, etc.

When working out criteria for *ex-post* evaluation, an important element in making them operational is to consider whether they may be scaled and if so what level would constitute satisfactory or successful performance. This goal may not be obtainable and, in this case, the evaluator has little choice but to standardize criteria by comparing one project with another. Comparison is an important tool but as in all social situations a perfect control is seldom obtained and great care needs to be exercised. Another dimension of comparison is with alternative methods of obtaining the programme objectives. Again, this is a powerful heurism but carries all the assumptions inherent in any hypothetical situation. For this reason this type of comparative technique is perhaps more appropriately applied before, rather than after, the research is funded.

Criteria for evaluation are, then, a combination of the objectives of the research programme and the purpose of the evaluation itself. Criteria pose the principal questions which the evaluation seeks to answer. In the next chapter we address the ways in which this answer is sought and the ways in which trade-offs between different criteria are resolved.

D.   ORGANISATION AND RESPONSIBILITY

In setting up an evaluation study it is wise to be clear about its scope, purpose and the criteria to be employed. But, in a sense, these elements constitute the intellectual or analytic side of the problem and though it is necessary that these be clarified this is far from being a sufficient condition for a successful evaluation. The social concomitant to the analytical task of getting the terms of reference straight is the organisation of the evaluation itself and, related to this, the delimitation of responsibility for carrying it out.

Perhaps the most important aspect of the whole exercise is the establishment of a framework of co-operation and collaboration between users of the evaluation and those being evaluated. As we have indicated previously, this phase of the study requires an attitude of openness on both sides and a willingness to explain why the evaluation is being carried out and how the results could be used. This is best done in dialogue rather than by *fiat* from above. It is the time to explain scope and purpose, to explore hidden agenda and to identify the evaluating team. This last is a frequently overlooked aspect of the evaluation of research. In evaluating scientific research the dialogue between the users and those being evaluated needs to identify the team of evaluators who are going to collect data, analyse it and report their findings. In evaluating narrow scientific specialities, for example, it might appear that the task is relatively straightforward: a group of experts drawn from the speciality itself and perhaps one or two from neighbouring areas of science. But as experience shows, this is a far from being a simple task, because even within a speciality it would be unusual to find a clear consensus as to where the future growth of the speciality lies.

The choice of evaluators is a crucial one. Some countries, particularly smaller ones, try to achieve a balance by leavening national representation on evaluation teams with a few foreign specialists. But, as the case of Sweden makes clear (see Chapter 4), this decision brings in its train the duty of explaining to foreign scientists the national context in which the particular research speciality exists. Even when a nationally-based team of evaluators is regarded as appropriate, considerable debate can take place in the dialogue between users and those to be evaluated before an acceptable choice emerges. For example, in some American universities the dialogue has taken the form of an internal list of suggestions for specialist departments being vetted by independent outside bodies before selection is made.

The choice of evaluators is a painstaking process but what is the point of carrying out an evaluation if at the end of it the impartiality of the evaluators is called into question? The problem of impartiality becomes more difficult to achieve as the research area to be evaluated becomes larger (i.e. involves more than one speciality) or becomes a different type (i.e. becomes more involved with social or economic goals). The broadening of the team of evaluators beyond the researchers to include industrialists, government officials and perhaps even members of the public creates a double problem. The first aspect of the problem concerns getting the right balance of expertise to consider a research programme or to evaluate the whole institute. Here, time and time again, it was revealed that evaluation teams, when they were composed of a broad range of specialists had considerable difficulty commenting effectively on the contributions made by the research to a set of social or economic goals. In most of the documentation that we have seen, it appears that far more attention was given to the results of the research than to whether or not the research was relevant to given programme objectives. This, we feel, is an intrinsic limitation of an evaluation team whose composition is decided primarily on the basis of relevant expertise. The second aspect of the programme lies in the education of non-specialist or lay members of research evaluation teams. It is a non-trivial problem for non-specialists to understand the information they are receiving and to use it effectively in the context of committee discussion and decision-making. Few countries, it seems, provide any training for lay members on evaluation teams. Broadening the representation often seems a good thing in its own right but as with the need to identify impartial specialists it is a necessary but not sufficient condition to achieve an effective evaluation of research.

There are two other elements which bear on the problem of organising an effective evaluation. The first concerns the procedures of evaluation. In the better evaluation studies one finds very clear guidelines given to the evaluating team which include the procedures to be followed from the beginning to the end of the study. Of course, they should be a matter of administration but in fact it often appears to be the case that the general purpose, scope and criteria for the evaluation are not translated into operational procedures that a group of evaluators could actually follow. If operational procedures are not worked out beforehand, then problems of comparability, interpretation, etc., arise at the synthetic stage and must reduce both the objectivity of the report and the weight which its recommendations will carry. The second problem is a structural one and concerns the question of the location of the evaluation in the relevant decision-making networks. The location will depend on whether the evaluation is a one-off study; whether it is an internal review, an external one or a mixture of the two; or whether it is part of a permanent ongoing evaluation. Whichever type of evaluation it may be, the evaluation team needs to be aware of the context in which its recommendations are likely to be used. Here we may consider the experience of French evaluation studies which reflect the difficulty of establishing a clear cut boundary between the internal and external environment. It is because this boundary may shift that the structure of evaluation needs to be clearly set up beforehand. Researchers will always fear that evaluations which are overtly wholly internal to their performance may later on play a role in the evaluation of a programme or an institution or even a whole discipline of science.

The organisation of evaluation – its structural features, procedures, the choice of evaluators, its degree of institutionalisation as permanent or *ad hoc*, the degree to which it is entirely an internal matter, etc., have distinct implications for the costs of carrying out evaluations. Two things have emerged in this respect from the experience of the country surveys. Firstly, evaluations are expensive, time consuming and frequently put pressure on the administration of research organisations to provide data which, though it exists, is not always in a form suitable for handing to the evaluation teams. Some indication of the cost of evaluation is given in Chapter 4. Secondly, evaluations are frequently seen as drawing scarce research resources into non-research purposes. The former is largely unavoidable, assembling expert groups who demand otherwise unorganised information is expensive; the latter problem, would be much alleviated if evaluation was presented as an investment in the research process and if separate budget lines were established from the outset for all major research programmes.

III. METHODS AND TECHNIQUES

In the preceding Chapter we have outlined what might be called some of the *precursors* to the evaluation of research. Questions of scope, purpose, criteria and organisation are *precursors* because they must be settled prior to and not during the study. Once these elements have been sorted out the way is open to choose the appropriate methods and techniques to achieve the objectives of the evaluation. It is perhaps worth explaining why the choice of methods and techniques was not included among the *precursors*. The principal reason is to emphasize the point that method must be in the service of the larger aims and objectives of evaluation not the other way round. In so doing, we hope to stress the danger – which arises from the growing sophistication of quantitative methods of evaluation of research – to set the scope, purpose and criteria for evaluation in relation to the availability of data. This, in our view, would be a mistake but more importantly it is also a source of worry to many of those charged with carrying out evaluations in ministries, universities and research councils that we have visited in the course of the study. In the development of techniques, an underlying factor has been that the available or easily measurable information, whatever it is, does not necessarily correspond to the criteria for evaluation, and hence methodological attention has concentrated on mediating between the two.

A. METHODS AND TECHNIQUES

It is useful to distinguish between methods (or approaches) and techniques of evaluation. There is currently one predominant method being employed to evaluate research and that method aims at a consensus of expert judgements. Within this broad category, it is possible to distinguish several different varieties of this method where the key to the differentiation lies in the amount of extra information the experts need to be supplied with in order to stand a reasonable chance of reaching a sound judgement. For example, a great number of evaluations in science use the peer review method. This approach assumes that, by and large, those passing judgement are in possession of the relevant information they think they need or if there is a lack in this respect it is clear how to obtain it. Such peer review assumes that the mere fact of being a recognised participant in a research area equips one with the basic information to make the relevant judgements. This type of information, while necessary, is not always regarded as sufficient to reach an expert judgement. If this is the case, the information base of peer review must be extended in a number of ways, for example, by obtaining a bibliometric information about the scientists or groups under scrutiny. Here, one is admitting into peer review objective data gathered for other purposes – that is publications and journals – and someone, usually not the peers themselves, has to collect the information. Peer review may be broadened further by gathering new information that reaches into and goes beyond the cognitive expertise of the peer review panels. For example, surveys of various kinds can establish whether users of research are satisfied with the results they have been given. Again, manpower and expertise is necessary to provide this information. Finally, information may be required which no-one in the peer review panel possesses. In other words the information may be the outcome of further research as when, for example, the experts need to know whether the benefits of research have exceeded (or are likely to exceed) costs. Here, other experts are asked to carry out a cost-benefit analysis and interpret its results.

In what follows, we examine the methods of evaluating research from the point of view of the amount and type of information which a peer review panel needs to carry out its job properly. Nonetheless, the fact remains that this method of evaluating research rests on the ability of the group of individuals to agree, to reach a judgement, about the outcome of a particular set of research activities. The method will break down if a collective agreement is not reached. Therefore, from the point of view of executing evaluation, one of the central problems is the management of the consensus forming activity. There is a growing amount of empirical evidence which shows a general tendency for consensus to break down when the organisational conditions for reaching it are not appropriate. In these cases, instead of communication and dialogue, review panels develop an adversarial mode of behaviour often structured along lines represented by the major cognitive interests on the panel. When this happens, the information so laboriously collected is turned away from its primary task of evaluation to discrediting the views or challenging the authority of fellow committee members. It follows from this that the drift into adversarial behaviour is likely to be more pronounced when a range of disciplines or a variety of goals must be accommodated in the final judgement. There is a distinct tendency, and the users of evaluation should be aware of this, for expert panels to reach consensus on what is non controversial and to leave the rest of the agenda to "higher" decision-making bodies. Such groups usually have even less detailed knowledge of the cases in question and so problems central to the evaluation of research become resolved by invoking one or other higher order objectives. From the point of view of the research group or the research institution, therefore, it often looks as if the decision has been taken on "political" grounds and when this happens the main elements of the evaluation – its scope, purpose and criteria – can be seen merely as a smoke screen to legitimate a prior decision. The problem unfortunately lies not with the elements but with the management of consensus in a situation where a range of viewpoints need to be accommodated.

From what has been said already, it will be clear that it is necessary to distinguish method from technique. Method will be used to describe various types of expert decision-making processes. Techniques will refer to different tools used to supply experts (i.e. evaluating teams) with information. In the context of the requirement for more precise information, each technique can be refined and part of this process is methodological. As with every other scientific technique, there is a more or less steady development of its *methodology*: that is the range of questions it can answer and those it cannot. Methodology, in this sense, does not question critically the decision-making processes which ultimately have to make use of the information collected and analysed by a given technique. It is important to note this because while we have uncovered a great deal of controversy over methodological aspects of certain techniques, there is at present little disagreement about the fundamental soundness of methods of evaluating research based on a consensus of experts.

In what follows, we present a brief critical review of the peer review method of evaluation together with a number of techniques which have been developed to supply further different types of information to the process of reaching consensus by experts. There is, in addition, a short commentary on what we have termed process evaluation and a final section is devoted to techniques for evaluating the economic and social impact of investments in research.

B. METHODS OF EVALUATION: PEER REVIEW

Peer review is the name given to the judgement of scientific merit by other scientists working in, or close to the field in question. Peer review is premised upon the assumption that a judgement about certain aspects of science, for example its quality, is an expert decision capable of being made only by those who are sufficiently knowledgeable about the cognitive development of the field, its research agenda and the practitioners within it. It is a social process which requires that a field be sufficiently large and cohesive for peers to possess this knowledge and that there has been sufficient time for the field to develop to the stage where a basis for agreement on what constitutes quality exists. In this section, three types of peer review, will be treated:

- *Direct peer review*: defined as review by a scientific peer or peers carried out specifically for the purpose of determining and confined to questions of scientific merit;
- *Modified direct peer review*: defined as the result of adjustments to direct peer review aimed at broadening the range of the criteria to be addressed;
- *Indirect peer review*: the use of historic peer review judgements made primarily for purposes other than the evaluation in question.

1. Direct peer review

This approach is present throughout the scientific enterprise. In terms of status, peer review is the most widespread and generally accepted method for reaching a judgement about the scientific quality of a proposal or group of proposals. At its simplest it involves seeking the views of an individual about the work of another. In form it may be no more than a letter of reference. The practice of refereeing is pervasive and controls the acceptance of papers by journals and conferences; it is also an important factor in appointment and promotion decisions. Many research project allocation systems rely on the views of one or more referees, even though the initial decision to consult referees may be taken by an official of even a committee. While referees are generally provided with guidelines or checklists to assist them in their appraisal, the success of the procedure is dependent upon the experience, ability and impartiality of those chosen. An important aspect of the process, then, is the choice of referees by editors, programme officials, etc. Care in selecting referees can, in most cases, eliminate the obvious forms of personal or institutional bias but there are cases where the nature of the field itself inhibits the proper operation of the peer review process. For example, when a proposal or group of proposals depart significantly from the prevailing orthodoxy, a choice of a referee may have a substantial effect on the decision made depending on whether the referee is broadly supportive of or intolerant of unorthodox views. On the other hand, empirical work on the factors affecting ratings for proposals carried out by the National Science Foundation found that while there was strong agreement on extreme cases, agreement was often less strong in the middle ground when referees were less sure of the innovative nature of claims being made by scientists seeking support (Cole *et al.*, 1981). A further limitation to the peer review process arises less from the degree of orthodoxy of the proposals than from the size of the field itself. In this regard, it has been argued that when a field is relatively small and facilities expensive, the impartiality of normal peer review is threatened because no member of the relevant discipline is unaffected by the decisions taken (Irvine and Martin, 1984). Finally, there is the view that peer review operates conservatively favouring the routine rather than the creative, the old over the young and men over women. Again, empirical support for this view is hard to come by. For example, in a recent study carried out by the National Science Foundation of the "fairness" of its decisions to potentially disadvantaged groups found that there was no significant bias in respect to age or sex of the proposers (NSF, 1982 and 1983).

Committee or group type peer reviews are common both for resource allocation and *ex-post* appraisal. In the former case the committees are constituted on a disciplinary basis usually with a view to covering the major facets of the discipline and with some kind of institutional balance. Almost always, membership is changed over a fixed period. The advantage of this is that individual biases will be of limited duration and that greater understanding of the review process will be diffused into the community. The disadvantage is that there may be lack of continuity of policy within the committee.

Committee members may reach decisions individually, through a group consensus or in a phased combination of the two. In the first case, some form of grading system is usually adopted to facilitate voting. In the assessment of proposals, the information inputs to the committee are the proposal documents, any background knowledge the members may possess, and possibly some preparatory analysis by the secretariat. The focus of appraisal may be on the project or the end use of the research or in some cases a combination of both.

Committees are also involved in *ex-post* appraisal, but less frequently so. In many allocation systems it is assumed that the granting cycle is sufficiently long to ensure that when applicants return for further funding, their peers will be aware of the results of their previous work. For this reason, committees are most frequently used in an *ex-post* context when the review involves a whole programme or institution. In these cases committees or panels inspect reports and publications from projects, interview researchers or visit the institution concerned. An *ex-post* evaluation exercise may be at the level of a review of a university department or a research centre or may extend to the whole laboratory or institute. In these cases, members are no longer strictly peers because they are obliged to make judgements which lie outside their discipline. A similar situation may arise when a committee has responsibility for a multi-disciplinary area. Here, we meet an intrinsic limitation of the direct peer review method; a difficulty of making strictly scientific judgements across specialities.

Limitation of direct peer review

The ideal state for peer review is a situation where resources are not severely constrained but where the decisions are made by a disinterested, single discipline panel solely on the basis of scientific merit. In the real world of science policy-making such purity is rarely, if ever, attained and, as a result, many criticisms of peer review arise out of how it behaves when it departs from ideal circumstances. For example, disinterestedness may be affected when a field is small or when expensive facilities involve the whole community. The problem of the size of various scientific communities is of particular importance for small countries where there may only be a limited number of researchers in a given field. A solution frequently adopted here is to add foreign scientists to the panel. A disadvantage of this approach is the lack of familiarity that foreign scientists are likely to have with the research system of the country in question. A variation on this theme has been to seek the views of expatriate scientists if they exist and are contactable in sufficient numbers. Resource constraints create serious difficulties for peer review systems. Most operate with some kind of grading system and function normally when all highly rated proposals receive funding. If resources are constrained, however, to the point where a selection has to be made from among highly rated proposals then the system is put under considerable strain for both panelists and researchers.

This situation is exacerbated considerably if peers are asked to make judgements between fields, either on multi-disciplinary committees or on higher level committees which are asked to allocate resources between fields. At a time of expanding budgets, historical allocations with some minor modifications tended to prevail. Where budgets are fixed or even in decline peers tend to act as advocates for their own specialities and in this case the committee's behaviour moves from a consensual to an adversary mode. Visiting panels may also be affected even if they are in single disciplines as they may be reluctant to undermine the position of their own field in the institution being evaluated. Indeed, there is some evidence to indicate that when gradings awarded by subject-based committees are compared with those gradings awarded by other higher level committees there is a tendency to "grade inflation" as committees begin to compete on behalf of their respective scientific fields (see Chapter 5).

2. Modified peer review

For strategic and applied areas of science, as well as for those cases where a broad view of science is required, criteria other than scientific merit must come into effect; notably, those concerning the socio-economic impact of the research or its potential for utilisation (i.e. external criteria must be considered). Normally, scientific expertise alone is not sufficient to make judgements of this kind and the direct peer review system has been adapted in various ways to deal with it. One approach, and it is the most frequently used, has been to include the users of research on committees and panels. Typically, the direct peer review system is expanded to include industrial scientists or engineers, scientific civil servants, etc., with the aim in view that their presence in decision-making will lead in the end to projects or programmes being evaluated by a broader range of scientific criteria. When this approach is working well, it can provide higher order (even political) decision-makers with a view in which scientific possibilities are related to the social, economic and political costs of attaining them. Arriving at such a balanced judgement is undoubtedly difficult but it must be attained if research funding is not to be determined entirely by political and financial expediency. Such balanced judgements are more likely to be attained if evaluations are carefully conceived in terms of their structure and organisation.

Different ways have been explored for dealing with this situation. The main thrust of these approaches is to separate scientific from broader social or economic considerations. For example, a method used in the Netherlands separates the criteria into sequential phases taking expert opinions in the first phase, then taking counter-comments from the proposers themselves in a second phase and finally putting the combined comments to a "lay jury" who then attempt to rate the proposals. Peer review can also be used as an advisory mechanism in research programmes where programme managers are in fact responsible for applying the external criteria. A well developed variation on this is used by the National Institutes of Health in the USA. Here, a dual review system for grant applications has been put in place in which a scientific review group provides an initial scientific review and makes budget but not funding recommendations. This review is followed by a second level in which a national advisory board (sometimes called a council) attempts to assess the quality of the first level scientific review, to make recommendations on funding, and to evaluate the programme priorities and advise on policy. In each of these cases, the application of external criteria are to a greater or lesser extent separated from questions of scientific merit. This has the advantage that whatever projects are funded they will first of all have passed the test of being judged "good science". A disadvantage is that separating the scientific from the social economic decision makes it difficult to know how the "relevant" good science is identified. In brief separated from the policy formulation stages and reduced to fulfilling an instrumental function only.

The direct peer review system can also be extended by interposing interviews and/or questionnaires as a technique that operates between a referees report and the anonymity of a committee. However, it has been argued that the social pressures acting on individual scientists when being interviewed inhibits a frank expression of views; this is particularly the case if the views expressed are adverse. For example, Martin and Irvine (1985) have developed a form of peer evaluation by conducting confidential interviews, using structured questionnaires, with third parties (i.e. scientists not involved directly in a peer panel). The technique which forms part of a larger evaluative programme based on converging partial indicators (see below) makes it possible to draw upon a larger sample of scientists than would ususally be represented on a peer review committee. This method, however, is relatively costly and requires skilled interviewers to be effective. It also relies on the interviewers providing an interpretation of the answers given in interviews which is not easy to check and which still has to be absorbed as a further item of information in the decision-making process. Many evaluators have suggested that this method of modifying traditional peer review procedures is, because of the way that the information is gathered, less reliable than straightforward open committee discussion in obtaining a balanced view when conflicting interests are involved.

3. Indirect peer review

In the previous section we have explored different modes of "opening up" the peer review process, the purpose of which was to gain better information about research performance. The first technique expanded the traditional panel or committee to the users of research, while the second made use of routine social science methods such as questionnaires and structured interviews to gather information about group or institutional performance in research. With this latter group of techniques, the evaluation of a specific discipline or field could be moved from the locus of a review committee to the relevant community of scientists as a whole; though it is an open question what use might be made of such information by others (that is, management, budgetary and legislative) structures. Indirect peer review takes this process of information gathering further in a quantitative direction. In this section we will examine some of the attempts that either have or are currently being made to gather quantitative information on research performance. These activities may be grouped into two general categories:

- Indicators based upon the reward system;
- Indicators based upon publications, sometimes known as *bibliometrics*.

Both approaches have long historical antecedents arising out of the propensity of scientists to measure their environment. However, it is only in the last two decades or so that a systematic attempt has emerged to apply quantitative indicators to evaluation. The most notable series of data relevant to evaluation has been the US National Science Board's series *Science Indicators* which began in 1972 and has consistently included bibliometric as well as other data. From a practical point of view an important work concerned with the application to bibliometrics to evaluation has been produced by Narin (1976) also for the US National Science Foundation. The following section seeks to review the main indicators which have emerged recently and to examine them selectively as tools for the evaluation of research. While the strengths and weaknesses of each are reviewed, the balance of coverage does not necessarily reflect the standing of those techniques. Some are covered because they are novel and emergent, some because they have been widely applied.

31

a) Indicators of the reward system

Distinction in scientific performance is recognised by the scientific community in many ways: through the award of prizes, membership of prestigious societies, of honorary degrees, and the like. These awards are part of the peer review system and provide a valid indicator of the approbation of one's peers but may also have a wider implication. For example, there is little doubt that receipt of Nobel prizes or a strong showing in other indicators creates a high standing for the institution in which the prize winners work. Counting such rewards is not difficult but two problems arise if they are to be applied as a measure of quality. First, the most prestigious awards are given for performance over an extended period and may relate to work long since completed. Second, the low level of incidence of many of these awards means that they are prone to statistical fluctuation even in the largest institutions. As Moravcsik (1985) has pointed out, awards of this kind are not strictly quantitative but rather represent a ranking of recipients. Certain other indicators do apply more widely and have been used in studies, for example, counting invitations to prestigious conferences. But it is sometimes argued that these sort of indicators are more a reflecting of the social organisation and "tribal customs" of different scientific sub-cultures than on the quality of the scientists *per se*. Evaluating and comparing these sort of indicators one with another is difficult without an extremely detailed and up to date knowledge of the sociology of the particular field.

Probably the indicator for which the best documented statistics exist is that of past funding decisions. This is commonly used as a measure of research performance particularly in university departments. In these cases, more weight is usually given to research funds that are based on the peer evaluation process rather than other sources as for example those which originate in an industrial or government contract. The principal objection to the more widespread use to this measure as an indicator of performance is that while it may be an output of the peer review process it is an input to research. The real evaluative question concerns the outcome of the use of the funds awarded.

b) Indicators based on publications: bibliometrics

Underpinning techniques which use publications in scientific journals as a source from which to derive evaluative information are three basic assumptions:

- That the output of scientific research is consistently represented by articles appearing in scientific journals;
- That the number of citations to these articles is a legitimate indicator of their impact or quality;
- That accurate data on these activities is available.

However, it is important to remember that scientists communicate the results in variety of ways only some of which may be recorded in the journals. Oral contributions, personal interactions, the "grey literature" of research reports, all provide channels for communications. Further, the more closely science is concerned with commercially or strategically significant areas, the more likely are its results to remain in a restricted domain and so not circulate freely through journal publications. Devotees of techniques based upon publication data counter that for the most basic science the only effect of mission-oriented work on publication patterns is to delay the publication and, therefore, only delay the possible impact of a piece of work. We cite these observations not to promote or deprecate indicators based on publication measures but to draw attention to the fact that the significance of publications in scientific journals is far from clear and that studies which use publication data must make assumptions as to that significance which may differ overtime as well as between fields. The published literature in science has no intrinsic relation to quality rather it is of importance for evaluation because it is a source to which scientists habitually look when they want to know what is going on in a given field.

c)   Publication counts

The most basic literature-based technique is the publication count, in which the number of publications by an individual, group or institution is aggregated. Publication counts constitute a key element in every evaluation and their use is widespread. While relatively easy to count, it is a much harder task to evaluate the significance of a given number of publications especially if the question of quality is involved. Most problems derive from the lack of criteria against which different types of publications can be ranked. These differences include multiple authorship, the possibility of publications being "spun out" to greater numbers in order to improve the author's tenure or promotion prospects, and the different standing of journals in which publications have been accepted. In certain circumstances it may not be possible to distinguish from the bibliometric information alone whether one is dealing say with articles, abstracts or reviews.

Publication is considered a necessary attribute for scientists (at the extreme it is sometimes referred to as the "publish or perish syndrome") and there seems to be a broad acceptance that more publications are better than fewer if only because they increase the chance of the work reaching other scientists and thus achieving an impact on the field. In some fields (for example defence research) there are limits put upon the number and type of publications. Thus publications as a measure become problematic where there are too many restrictions on the freedom to publish. This may for example be restricted by patent requirements. It has been suggested that the number of technical reports produced by industrial or defence scientists could provide a quality or impact measure but without the editorial control exercised upon publications the problem of comparability is exacerbated.

Despite these limitations, techniques based upon publication counts continue to develop both in the quality of data on which a subsequent analysis will be based and in the precision with which the group to be evaluated can be identified. For example, publication counts can be tied more firmly to the peer review element in publication by examining the numbers of accepted articles in the three top journals in a particular field. This technique has been used at the institutional, departmental and individual levels in some evaluation studies. At the institutional level, Narin (1985) has used this type of publication count to provide a profile of an institution. Here the measure used is called an "activity index" which is the proportion of an institution's papers in a given field divided by the proportion of all papers in the data base in the same field. Analytically, this has the effect of normalizing the publication count for the size of the institution and the size of the field. The latter may avoid some of the problems encountered when different fields exhibit different propensities to publish. If the publications used also acknowledge sources of research support, this method can be extended to provide information about funding agencies and thus make it possible to get an estimate on the impact of particular funding policies. A further development of this idea has been used by the same author in some work for the United States National Institutes of Health. This involves identifying the "research level" (Narin and Gee, 1980) of the research groups publications. The *Science Citation Index* classifies journals into four levels according to a scale ranging from basic research (level four) to clinical investigation of applied research (level one). This may be used to characterise the work of an institution by examining the proportion of publications in each category. This technique has to be used with care because it relies on adequate classifications of journals and does not work very well when journals cannot be unambiguously associated with the particular level. To some extent this problem can be reduced if levels are defined by their relation to a specific "prototype journal", though clearly this will depend on the degree of cognitive development of each particular field.

d) Citation analysis

Given some of the limitations of publication counts, much of evaluative bibliometrics has been focused upon citation analysis. This technique rests upon the fact that scientists cite earlier publications because the work contained in them is, in some way, relevant to their own. Here, a critical assumption is that the number of citations reflect the influence of an article relative to others and, in this way, the quality of scientific research can be measured. A precondition for this technique to work is that data of sufficient scope and quality with which to calculate accurately the number of citations in a given instance be available. For all the evaluations we have encountered this data base has been supplied by the *Science Citation Index*.

Arguments for and against citation techniques concern the significance of the act of citation, the representativeness of the data and the degree to which the results agree with other measures. The limitations of citation analysis have been extensively reviewed, for example by Moed *et al.* (1983) and by Moravcsik (1985). The basis of criticisms about citation behaviour rests on the belief that not all citations are made for cognitive reasons. Excessive citations to oneself and one's friends, of papers or individuals favoured by an editor or others in positions of power, prestige citing and citations made to legitimate a paper represent some possible departures from the ideal that citations simply reflect contributions to the knowledge base of a particular paper. There are further limitations. For example, Moravcsik (1985) has argued that conceptual contributions soon become untraceable while new methods and tools continue to be cited and accumulate large citation scores. In addition, "negative" citations – papers cited because they are thought to be incorrect – provide another potential source of error when simple citation counting is used. Some of the limitations on the use of citation analysis can be avoided if it is known whether or not the citation behaviour is consistent. This is more likely to be the case within the field where publication occurs in the same journals and the citation practice, whatever it is, is accepted. Finally, any analysis must allow a sufficient length of time for paper to achieve an impact. Opinions differ but the average length of time for paper to have an impact, if it is going to have one, is usually between 3 and 5 years after publication.

Questions concerning the integrity of the data include problems such as the coverage of the data base. The *Science Citation Index* (SCI) includes approximately 3 000 journals, which is estimated as being under 10 per cent of the total number. However, 75 per cent of citations are accounted for by 1 000 journals so coverage of this indicator is high. A principal criterion for inclusion of a journal by SCI is the number of citations it receives. This varies according to field, being good for most natural and life sciences but weaker in such areas as psychology. A common criticism is that the journal coverage shows a bias towards English language publication and may discriminate against those publishing primarily in other languages. From the point of view of those using the index in evaluation studies, considerable care need to be taken because the index may contain errors. For example, the index lists first authors only and does not adequately distinguish between homonyms. These problems are generally considered to be surmountable through manual checking and "cleaning up" of the data base prior to an analysis is frequently necessary.

A variety of techniques has been devised to exploit the citation data base, both as a descriptive and an evaluative tool. The simplest one is "citation frequency", the number of times the paper has been cited. This can be aggregated for authors, institutions or countries.

For the reasons outlined above, if its results are to be at all meaningful, this method must involve careful comparison with similar groups to whom the same constraints apply. One method of calibrating citation frequencies of a unit is to compare them with the average citation counts to all publications in the journals in which the unit has published. This is called the "expected impact" indicator (Moed *et al.*, 1985). Trend analysis may also be applied though care must be taken to ensure that the data base, or the basic conditions within the field, remained the same during the period. In an attempt to provide comparability across fields or through time an indicator known as "top decile performance" has been developed. This indicator is defined as the fraction of a set of papers in a field and it is claimed that this statistic is of real relevance in the identification of "world class" science (Narin, 1985). Questions which have been raised concern the justification of the figure of 10 per cent, the effective different distributions between fields and whether the highly cited papers that do emerge are indeed the most important. Citation frequency analysis is inevitably a slow process since it takes time – one to three years – for citations to accumulate and the intricate task of processing citations adds a further year. A short cut method has been developed which, in certain circumstances, can drastically reduce the time (Pinski and Narin, 1976). This technique is the concept of journal influence and is based upon the assumption in that a citation from a more influential journal is worth more than one from an obscure journal and that a journal's influence is related to the number of citations the papers in it receive. Using a set of journal influence weights calculated in 1973, it is possible to assess lists of published papers according to the journals in which they appear. This is a relatively simple exercise producing up to date results. Its main disadvantages are that the technique assumes that all papers in a journal are of the same quality and thus it lacks the ability to discriminate between them. Furthermore, journal influence weights change over time (as do the titles available) and so relatively recent weightings are required for the best results.

An alternative approach to citation analysis has been developed in Canada (MacAuley, 1985). This technique is founded in information theory and calculates the conditional probability that given an author makes a reference to any given paper, he will, in the same article, make references to any other specific paper in the whole source of cited papers. It is claimed that this technique allows the identification of directional pathways which point out the most influential papers. The measure is formalized in a mathematical concept called "relevance" (*viz.* the relevance of any cited paper to all other cited papers). The technique is not affected by bias arising from prestige or self-citings. Problems with it lie, firstly, in whether the techniques are valid and secondly, in its lack of transparency. For example, relevance is a term which occurs frequently in the context of evaluation but the technical term is not identical with what it is conventionally understood to signify. As far as we are aware, this technique is not diffused widely either within Canada or elsewhere.

e)   Techniques using relational indicators

While publication counts in citation frequency analysis are essentially concerned with productivity, a second group of measures use similar data in what Rothman (1985) has termed relational studies. Primarily qualitative, these seek to identify networks of scientists or publications which represent the relationship between researchers, institutions or specialities. They are considered to be techniques for evaluation because *ex-ante* they identify emerging areas of research which can, for example, assist in deciding upon priorities, while *ex-post* they allow the position of an institution or even a country to be established relative to the main thrust of the field. What all these methods have in common is the use of a cluster analysis algorithm to represent and interpret the results they yield. The principal advantage of these approaches is that, unlike productivity studies, they do not rely upon externally imposed category walls between disciplines of fields. As these categorisations often form the units of analysis for other subsequent comparisons such as funding or output, this is of considerable significance for evaluations. The problem of *a priori* categorisations is they are often developed for institutional reasons and are not consistent within and, especially, between countries. Furthermore, the rapidly developing science means that some of the categories can become dated in a very short period. Relational techniques use the cluster approach to identify groupings which correspond to a research theme. With suitable measures of distance from the theme not only will the categories emerge but the relation to other categories will also become apparent. A simple relational approach is based upon citations between journals. The more citations between any two particular journals, the stronger are their links. Cluster analysis can be used to produce maps of fields to the extent that journals correspond to some fields. Multi-disciplinary journals present a problem here particularly where these are prestigious and highly cited.

f) Co-citation techniques

That there is some form of link between two papers which cite the same reference is undeniable but until recently it has not been possible to draw meaningful results from this primarily because there has been no way of gauging the strength of that link and hence distinguishing close relationships from casual ones. To avoid this problem an approach has been developed initially by Henry Small, which uses co-cited papers; that is to say, that if two papers are cited together in a paper by a third party they are deemed to have a link with the strength of one unit. Each time they are co-cited by other papers in the literature data base the strength of the cognitive link is increased by one unit. Highly co-cited papers are considered to be the "core" or "base" literature of a research theme or cluster. The current literature citing these core publications can then be assembled into clusters. Papers from the current literature may refer to (and thus be clustered with) more than one core. A series of refinements or additions can be made to tailor this approach to specific needs. A fairly simple version developed by White and Griffith (1981) used authors rather than papers as the basic unit of analysis. Since co-citation is computationally cumbersome and hence expensive, it is common to preselect a target literature data base, perhaps based upon journals known to be in the field of question and papers citing articles in them.

Institutions or nations can use the co-citation technique to identify the extent to which they are producing or citing core publications. One application which has been used to a restricted extent by some Member countries employs co-citation techniques when considering international collaborations as a means of identifying strengths and gaps in potential partners. With this technique a time series approach is possible which illustrates dynamic changes in research patterns.

A new approach using fractional citation counting has been put forward by Small and Sweeney (1985) which aims to avoid biases against fields with fewer publications and/or reference lists. The solution offered is to give each citing item a total voting strength of one but to divide it among all references it cites. This does not of course, avoid the problem that citations in reality may widely vary in weight. Typically, selection of the threshold at which to model clusters was at a level which happened to yield the best results. Various automatic techniques are being developed to optimise this process. Perhaps the most important criticism of a technique whose main application is probably in *ex-ante* evaluation of priorities is that it has an inherent time lag of at least three years and hence the research hot spots it identifies may have been superseded by the time the analysis is available.

Rothman (1985) has reviewed the main drawbacks of the co-citation methodology which may be summarised as follows:

- Lack of adequate coverage of technology;
- Expensive and laborious models;
- Sociological and cognitive objections to citation analysis;
- Differences in citation practices between fields;
- Arbitrary selection of thresholds.

Much current academic work is addressing these problems but it is likely to be some time before reliable analyses become routinely available. Before this happens the expense and laboriousness will have to be reduced by increased automation of the analysis using improved computer software.

The clusters which emerge in a co-citation analysis are best examined and interpreted by experts in the field, providing a link between this technique and peer review. In one application of the technique (van Heerigen, 1985) a criticism raised was that some clusters were so small that they were not discernible.

Other relational approaches

The group of techniques known as co-word analysis originating and developed largely in France, seeks to derive cognitive networks from the words used by scientists in identifying their work. It remains experimental but development is continuing in France and the UK. Specifically, co-word analysis uses the words professional indexes ascribe to articles when compiling the bibliographic data bases. Papers are linked with the degree of co-occurrence of their key words (Turner *et al.*, 1985). The starting point is to identify the frequencies of the key words most often used in the documents. A document in this method need not be a journal article but may also include a report or a patent, thus allowing the technique to be extended into technological areas. The output of the analysis is a co-occurrence matrix relating key words and from these a series of calculations examine the significance of the word associations. Criticisms of the approach have focused on whether indexes use the same terms as the authors whose papers they describe and whether taking only the most frequent terms would prevent emergent areas from being detected. In response, proponents of the technique are developing computer assisted indexing and an approach studying the changes in word lists over time to identify emerging areas.

A technique known as co-nomination which is under development in the UK uses questionnaires sent out to researchers as the data input for a clustering exercise. Researchers are asked to nominate a list of scientists whose work is most familiar or relevant to their own and to identify the nature of the relationship, that is whether theory or equipment or method constitutes the primary linkage. They are also asked to name their own collaborators so that links between research groups can be readily identified. The disadvantage of this technique are that it is too laborious to be used in very large scale exercises and that it could be manipulated by those questioned. Its advantages are that it allows the inclusion of industrial scientists who are less likely to appear in strictly literature-based surveys. This type of method is particularly useful when an assessment of the use and extent of collaborative links between research groups is important.

g) *Comparisons of direct and indirect peer review methods*

Claims for the bibliometric and other indirect methods have tended to rest upon the degree to which they yield results similar to direct peer rankings. The early research literature on bibliometrics generally found high correlations between numbers of citations and rewards (scientific honours, etc.) on direct assessment by peers [Cole and Cole (1967) and Narin (1976, 1980, 1985)]. Few would disagree that there is a correlation; each manifests different aspects of the same system of judgements. There appeared to be more difficulties when the two are compared individual cases. For example, in the US Department of Energy, panel ratings assigned to a large sample of projects in the Basic Energy Sciences Program did not show a significant correlation. The errors and variations in the system seem to make citation unsuitable for the appraisal of individual scientists or projects without careful checking and interpretation by peers familiar with the context of the judgement. In consequence it is unlikely that bibliometric approaches will be adopted in project selection decisions except as an *additional* item of information for evaluators to consider. Their role, in methodological terms, appears to be in aggregated, *ex-post* reviews, particularly of basic science and there again as one element to be taken into account among others, as a tool for evaluators not an evaluation *per se*.

Converging partial indicators

Taking as a starting point the view that bibliometric and other indicators are partial and imperfect, each reflecting a slightly different facet of research performance, Martin and Irvine (1985) have developed an approach which seeks to combine them. Essentially, the methodology looks for a convergence between these partial indicators; when they all point in the same direction, they are also regarded as reliable. The basis of the methodology is comparative, examining carefully matched research groups, often in the big sciences with similar facilities pursuing similar research. Matching, here, is intended to compensate for variation and publication and citation rates.

In addition to publication and citation counts, this method uses direct evaluation based upon interviews with peers who are asked a range of questions aimed at ranking the institutions under comparison. This last measure is, of course, highly dependent upon the sample chosen and the nature of the interview conducted. The authors of the technique have noted that they "use verbal rather than written surveys in order to press an evaluator if a divergence between expressed opinions and actual views is suspected" (Martin and Irvine, 1985). Further criticism of the methodology is centred upon the dimensions of matching that have been employed. Matching requires congruence not only in terms of scientific field but also, especially with big science facilities, the stage in the equipment cycle and the context in which the institution is situated. More fundamentally, if the indicators are measuring different facets of the same process (i.e. peer review) then it may not be important whether or not they converge because, according to the methodology, if the indicators do not converge they are not reliable. Moreover, the time frame in which the observations are made may significantly affect the balance between the peers. Despite these criticisms, the applications of this method to radioastronomy and CERN have aroused considerable interests and debate, albeit that the exercises have been primarily academic.

C. THE METHOD OF PROCESS EVALUATION

Process evaluation adresses quite different issues from either *ex-ante* review, *ex-post* evaluation of output or evaluations concerned with economic outputs which will be discussed in the next section. It is concerned with the structures and mechanisms of research and it is most often applied at the programme or at the institutional level. At its simplest, process evaluation comes close to formal monitoring of the sort that is used throughout industry and government. Process evaluation is primarily concerned with managerial performance; in the way in which programmes are executed. It seeks to derive operational indicators such as the speed of processing proposals or the pattern of budget allocations and to judge the efficiency of these processes.

Where process evaluations are at their most useful is in the context where the research has a complex or innovative structure or where several interfaces are involved such as those that might exist between universities or government laboratories and industry. The interest in this technique is because it is felt that these aspects of R&D are potentially transferable between programmes.

The process evaluation, then, sets out to examine the effectiveness of these structures. The issues may include the functioning of advisory or peer review mechanisms or the state of linkages between the research groups. Typically an evaluation of this type would draw upon interviews, documentation and formal surveys and unlike output measures, the question of effective working of processes can often be addressed while the programme is still running. An example described in Chapter 6 is the evaluation of the UK's Alvey Programme.

A method, sometimes called the audit method or the method of unstructured interviews has recently attracted attention[2]. This method consists of the collection of information through field interviews with various interested parties. Let's take for example:

"an audit of a research institution or technical centre: a group of investigators (in general up to 10) will be commissioned to perform this task. The group will be headed by a chairman designated by the supervisory ministry, the terms of reference being indicated in a letter drafted in very general terms. This group will organise interviews with a certain number of persons depending on the size of the organisation being examined. The persons interviewed belong mostly to the organisation but also to its clients and suppliers (interface) and to the supervising administrations. This work requires time, in general many months, and is concluded by the drafting of a report of the group which is submitted to the supervisory ministry as well as to the managers of the organisation which was audited[2]."

This method is seen to have the obvious merit of flexibility in that new questions can be raised and problems tackled as the audit proceeds.

"However, this type of flexibility means that the outcome of the audit will be extremely sensitive to the composition of the auditing group and to the personality of the group's chairman. The audit method is used unevenly among OECD Member countries except perhaps in France where the method was used extensively by the Cour des Comptes for examining management of public funds and by various ministries for examining public research centres. Indeed, from the information collected from Member countries, the audit seems to be most often used to evaluate the performance of research organisations or technical centres[2]."

By contrast with the type of audit described in the previous paragraph in which a group descends upon an organisation, gathers information and writes a report is the example of the evaluation which is being conducted experimentally within the United Kingdom's Alvey Programme. In the Alvey Programme for advanced information technology research, the evaluation (or audit) is being carried out in real time; that is, the evaluators report as the programme proceeds and at the same time accumulate data for an *ex-post* exercise, thus meeting the common problem of distortion caused by hindsight.

It should be noted that a real time evaluation is not the same as monitoring a programme. Monitoring is a process whereby programme managements or sponsors can obtain information as to its progress the emphasis being descriptive rather than analytical (Gibbons, 1984). While the process approach is more general and does not constitute a given set of techniques, it addresses issues which are often critical to the success of the programme under study; for example, there are unlikely to be industrial benefits from a university programme if the linkages are not functioning effectively. Process evaluations can be part of *ex-post* peer review exercises but generally they are too time consuming to be undertaken in the short period normally available to members of such committees and they require at least the support of a team of full-time evaluators. High level science policy reviews often address process-type questions as part of their remit. In so far as there is a relationship between the structure and management of programmes or institutions and their output, process evaluation provides a useful additional approach.

D.   EVALUATION OF ECONOMIC AND SOCIAL IMPACT

A significant proportion of research is directly justified in terms of the benefits which are expected to accrue to society as a result of it. The time-scale within which the benefits are expected to flow and the degree to which a direct link is intended *a priori* varies according to the position of the research on the spectrum from basic through strategic to applied research. Nonetheless, economic justification is necessary and even occurs in arguments in support of basic research. In these cases it is essential to distinguish between science as a consumption activity and science as an investment activity (see Metcalfe, 1985). The principal problems in evaluating research from the point of view of investment are threefold: first, research by its nature is uncertain and by no means all of it will (or should) lead to measurable benefits (this is particularly a problem for those engaged in *ex-ante* evaluation); second, even if the benefits are clear the time-scale is often very long, implying that if the evaluation is delayed until some tangible effect is discernible the results will come too late to have significant impact on policy; and third, that for economic benefits to arise there needs to be successful innnovation; and the processes by which knowledge generated by research is transferred to new products in process is complex. As a consequence input-output models which do not attempt to enter the black box but simply try to correlate investment levels in science with other macro-economic outputs are unlikely to produce convincing results.

Not surprisingly, then, many impact evaluations stop short of a full economic appraisal. The approach most commonly adopted then is the user-evaluation, that is the identification of the users of research results say industry or social agencies and the seeking of their views as to its usefulness. Interviews, postal and telephone surveys, etc., are used in more systematic studies, while high level enquiries tend to take evidence from parties which have or declare an interest (see the discussion of audits in the previous section). The Fraunhofer Institute in the Federal Republic of Germany, in evaluating government funding and promotion of R&D and innovation in small and medium-sized firms, has used this approach but expressed the results quantitatively in an indicator referred to as the "innovation intensity" (defined as the sales contribution made by new products) of a firm (Meyer-Krahmer, 1982). Some other approaches are outlined below.

1.   Techniques to assess the impact of research

Case studies still represent one of the most useful techniques for examining the relationship between research and its economic or social impact. When these are carried out in sufficient numbers and in sufficient detail they represent probably the best chance of fully identifying the relationships involved. The problem from the point of view of evaluation of research is how to generalise from the sample selected. By themselves, case studies are expensive to carry out and are time consuming and require very careful methodological preparation if they are to be effective in evaluating the impact of research.

A variant on the case study approach developed originally in the United States in the 1960s and exemplified in the Hindsight and TRACES projects are being invoked again by the Office of Naval Research in the USA and by the Science and Engineering Research Council in the UK. The object of these techniques is to trace out historically the development from research to application or vice versa and to try and identify the major events which link the former with the latter. For example, the role of sponsored research that contributed to the Trident submarine has been identified. These techniques suffer from the difficulties of using a simple linear model as the heuristic assumption in selecting and structuring the data. The original method was heavily criticised (Kreilkamp, 1971), because it led to a reconstruction of a sequence of events between which a causal connection was falsely presumed to exist; because the events identified were incorrectly given equal weight; and because historical dead ends were ignored; and because the results were sensitive to the selected time frame. Nonetheless, these types of approaches highlight the complexity of the problem faced by evaluators who seek an economic justification for basic and strategic research and, therefore, direct attention critically to the assumptions on which economic and other quantitative models are based.

Going a stage further there are techniques associated with cost-benefit analysis and its variants, developed primarily for investment appraisal. Also in this category are econometric techniques based upon a production function approach. In theory these techniques are appropriate but it is hard to get the necessary data and to identify in a sufficiently robust way the externalities arising from research; that is to say the benefits not captured in the price. Furthermore, the same piece of research may yield in addition benefits which are not quantifiable on the same basis, for example the educational benefits, greater industrial awareness, etc. Together with techniques such as Delphi exercises, relevance trees and decision analysis these methods find their widest application in rather broad brush *ex-ante* reviews and priorities. A possible exception is agricultural research where research on some varieties is extremely specific and where benefits can be captured by a single indicator, say improved yield, with a reasonable accuracy assuming there are no price effects as a result. As far as we have been able to discern cost-benefit type analyses are not used very much in evaluating research – at least as far as the Member countries are concerned.

2. Technology indicators

Occupying a role similar to that of publication count analysis in basic science is the use of patent statistics as indicators of technological performance; that is to say an extensive data base is available but there are dangers in regarding them as the sole output of research. Freeman (1982) has reviewed some of the difficulties. Firstly, patents do not arise uniquely from industrial R&D nor is it a measure of failure if these latter do not lead to patentable results. Publications can and do arise from applied research. Furthermore, patents are a measure of intermediate output – they do not necessarily result from previously patented knowledge. Perhaps the most important caveat about the use of patents as a performance indicator is that firms have variable propensities to patent and these may change over time. Secrecy is often chosen as the best method of protecting intellectual property rights which after all is the end purpose of a patent. Together with criticisms – identified by the OECD 1980 Science and Technology Indicators Conference – that patent data differ qualitatively, these constitute the main arguments against the use of patents as an evaluative tool. Whether it is due to the perceived limitations of the patent record or not, the use of patents has tended to remain at a higher aggregated level; for example, in comparisons of national performance or at the industry level (Pavitt, 1982). One study which did not attempt to use patents for an evaluation of research was carried out by the US National Science Foundation in 1982. This study aimed to determine the extent to which the National Science Foundation's Chemistry Program led to patented technology to estimate the economic value of those patents and to develop a systematic method of evaluating patents associated with other NSF research support grants. The study found that, between 1964 and 1967, one per cent of grantees produced patents related to the grants (based upon acknowledgements to NSF support or subjective judgements) and that aggregate long-term sales of products derived from those patents was of the magnitude of $20-30 million. The economic value of patents was estimated by dispatching a questionnaire to holders ascertaining facts as to whether it was licensed and so forth.

The issue of variation in the quality of patents has been addressed by looking at citations to patents, and data bases now exist to allow this in some countries. Citations of patents to scientific literature provide another source. Freeman (1982) in reviewing this work concluded that much remains to be done in the study of referencing behaviour patterns in various countries before patent citations can be used with as much confidence as literature citations.

To avoid reliance on patents as indicators of technical change, methods are being developed for direct measurements of technical change using a characteristics approach (Saviotti and Metcalfe, 1982). This has potential for evaluation and is the subject of a study for the UK Department of Trade and Industry as a method for identifying technological priorities. Its application to specific R&D programmes is limited by the fact that characteristics are determined by an interaction between the technology and the market and not by research and development alone.

Overall, the status of technology indicators appears to be that they are gaining ground as policy tools but before they can be effectively used in the broad range of R&D evaluations a better understanding of the means by which knowledge enters the economy is necessary. The role of new technologies of communication may be of crucial importance in this area, in establishing and maintaining networks in science and providing advanced software to help decision-making.

IV. ADMINISTRATION OF EVALUATION

As Chapter 2 stressed, the organisation of an evaluation is one of the key elements which define the evaluation and its outcome. In this Chapter, some of the themes discussed there will be addressed in the light of the experience of Member countries. In the first Section, the degree of centralisation of evaluation within government is discussed; in Section B the choice of evaluators is considered; and in Section C an important organisational issue, the cost of evaluation, is addressed.

A. CENTRALISATION

1. Frameworks for evaluation

The ways in which evaluation is approached in the Member countries reflects the political and administrative culture of those concerned. Thus, in the USA, characterised by a pluralistic decentralised research support system, there are no standard procedures which agencies must follow (other than, as in all the countries studied, the basic procedures necessary to satisfy accountability requirements for public funds). However the process by which budgets are appropriated by Congress has led to an interest there in evaluation of research and calls for more independent quantitative measures of the output from research.

France, however, which has a long tradition of planning, has only recently institution-alised procedures for the evaluation of major national programmes launched at ministerial level: technological development programmes, programmes for the implementation of the Guideline and Programming Act (1982).

Programme planning and evaluation in fact takes place at two different institutional levels: that of the research organisations (CNRS, INSERM, etc.) which, by virtue of their status and from their inception, were equipped with scientific evaluation bodies, and that of the major programmes involving a number of ministries and various social and economic partners (universities, firms, government agencies).

In particular, the Law Relating to Research and Technological Development of 23rd December 1985 (No. 85.1376) stresses the importance of the evaluation of programmes launched at ministerial level in achieving economic and social objectives through the contribution of science and technology. Evaluation is considered to be particularly important for measuring programme spin-off in scientific and social and economic terms. The Law indicates that an evaluation would first be carried out two years after the start of the programme and then every three years. Apart from making it clear that this approach should supplement the present system of assessing personnel, the Law does not seek to lay out particular methodological approaches, stressing instead that evaluation needs to be adapted to the specific nature of each programme. It should not be limited to scientific aspects, but should extend to the strategic and operational issues with use of appropriate objective indicators and attention paid to technology transfers effected by the research organisations.

Also, it is provided that the minister responsible for Research and Technological Development should submit to Parliament an annual report covering the main aspects of research activity.

Further evidence of the central commitment to evaluation is shown by the Ministry of National Education which has established a National Evaluation Committee consisting of fifteen members appointed for four years (nine scientists and four with economics and research qualifications) to prepare an annual report on the workings of universities. Working through expert *ad hoc* commissions, including external experts, the Committee carries out audits. The actions of these two ministries indicate that a framework for evaluation has been put in place in France in recognition of earlier deficiencies in this area.

The "building in" of a requirement for evaluation has also been effected in the research activities of the European Communities. Under Council resolution of 28th June 1983 on a Community plan of action relating to the evaluation of Community research and development programmes, earlier experimental approaches were extended to a broad range of Community R&D. Evaluations take place approximately midway through each four or five year programme taking into account the results of the previous programme and the partial results of the current programme. More details are given in Chapter 7. A requirement to submit the reports to various Community bodies is accompanied by an injunction to disseminate reports to other interested organisations, particularly potential users of research results in the industrial or other sectors. In the current proposed Framework Programme of Technological Research and Development 1987-1991, the Commission intends to strengthen both its internal continuous monitoring activities and the evaluations performed by external independent peers. Furthermore this programme foresees research on evaluation methodology and the creation of a European network in the field of R&D evaluation. The importance of socio-economic impact assessments has been repeatedly stressed by several Member States.

Perhaps the most extensively defined and widely applied central framework for evaluation is that operating in Canada. As part of a general trend towards increased accountability in government, the Treasury Board issued a Policy on "Evaluation of Programs by Departments and Agencies" in 1977. At that time there was little formal programme evaluation. The Office of the Comptroller General (OCG) was created to improve management practices and controls, including the establishment of a programme evaluation function in each government department and agency. The Office comments on the quality of evaluations and has issued a set of principles and a guide. These documents provide a reference point against which evaluations in each department may be designed and assessed, given variations demanded by the particular situation. The general approach to evaluation is applied to the specific instance of the evaluation of research and experimental development programmes.

The basic style formulated by OCG is present in all *ex-post* evaluations carried out in government. *Ex-ante* evaluation is much more the province of the individual department or agency, reflecting the different needs imposed by their functions. Thus in the Natural Sciences and Engineering Research Council (NSERC), responsible for funding scientific research in universities, a well developed peer review system is in operation while in the mission-oriented agencies selection of priorities and projects is far more a management function. *Ex-post* evaluation has been built into the administrative structure of departments, with a requirement that the deputy head of each department or agency is responsible for establishing the evaluation function and acting as client for the evaluation. Internalising the process in this way, is intended to maximise its effect as an aid to decision-making and management, essentially as an information input. Explicitly eschewed is the notion of evaluation as an independent experimental research exercise designed to identify and measure the results of the government interventions in society. Objectivity remains a priority and is the reason that responsible for programme evaluation is distinguished from internal audit which addresses the efficiency of internal management practices while evaluation is concerned with programme structure and results.

OCG does not try to impose the specific issues to be addressed upon the departments as it believes these should be structured to relate to the decision-making in those departments. However, it has identified four generic issues which should be addressed by all evaluations. These are:

- Programme rationale (does the programme make sense?);
- Impacts and effects (what has happened as a result of the programme?);
- Objectives achievement (has the programme achieved what was expected?);
- Alternatives (are there better ways of achieving the results?).

A further co-ordination mechanism in Canada is provided by the Ministry of State for Science and Technology which presents an annual Framework Paper to Cabinet.

B.   CHOICE OF EVALUATORS

1.   Peer review

Chapter 3 described some ways in which the peer review system can be modified by the choice of who is involved. But how is that choice made? In most countries it falls either to existing committees to co-opt new members, or else to the Secretariat responsible for administering the programme. The choice of referees for proposals is a powerful instrument which relies on the confidence of the scientific community to ensure its proper use. Where the organisation is commissioning an evaluation of its own activities it is particularly important that the evaluators are seen to be objective and hence that the process by which they are selected is too. One way in which this objectivity may be obtained is through the use of foreign scientists. The evaluation process operated by the Swedish National Research Council (see Chapter 5) always includes foreign experts in evaluation teams and attaches considerable weight to their judgements. The tension is between objectivity and finding experts with sufficient knowledge of the country to perform a useful evaluation. This has been the experience of the German Research Association (DFG), an autonomous body that promotes and supports science, particularly basic research. Reviewers in the main programme are nominated by their scientific and learned societies and elected by secret ballot for a four-year term of office by all their colleagues active in university or other non-profit research institutions who have held a doctorate for more than three years. From the 450 reviewers elected in this way are drawn most of the members of the *ad hoc* committees which evaluate the special collaborative programmes (see Chapter 5). However, while there is a deliberate attempt to get international evaluators to participate in the group, in recent years only 3-5 per cent have been from abroad. This has been partly explained by the fact that the language used both in the publications and during the site visits is, naturally, German.

2. Professional evaluators

A trend in recent years has been the emergence of professional evaluators, that is, people whose prime function is to carry out evaluation, unlike the "part-timers" of the peer review system. Two main groups may be identified:

- Evaluators within the organisation; and
- Independent evaluators (including those working under contract).

Professional evaluators are rarely an alternative to peer review, indeed organisations which function primarily by peer review also have evaluation offices. For example, in the USA both the National Science Foundation and the National Institutes of Health have staff carrying out evaluation activities on a permanent basis. The functions of professional evaluators differ from peer review in several respects: first, the prime concern is with *ex-post* evaluation; second, the level of aggregation is higher; and third, the issues addressed are often different. Quality is addressed, through surveys, panels or commissioned bibliometric analysis, all of which require logistic support. Other functions include servicing the peer review system, checking it for fairness and analysing trends in judgements. It also often falls to professional evaluators to address the social or economic impact of programmes. The advantages of having evaluators within an organisation are that they will be able to build up considerable expertise and "inside knowledge". Also there is scope for the evaluation to be carried out on a routine basis and for the results to be an integral part of the decision-making process. The interface between the evaluators and other parts of the organisation is one which needs careful handling to maintain confidence in the evaluation and secure co-operation on the one hand, and to protect the integrity and security of the evaluators on the other. One example of an interface arrangement is found in the UK Department of Trade and Industry. There, co-ordination is carried out through the Evaluation Working Group (EWG) which was established to provide a coherent basis for programme evaluation work taking account of all department programmes. It is also responsible for ensuring divisions prepare proper plans for monitoring and evaluation, and for dissemination of findings. A checklist for evaluations is supplied. The EWG synthesises important findings, helping to redraft summaries to relate to policy issues of concern as evaluators themselves may be unaware of these. The evaluation programme is prepared on a rolling year-by-year basis and submitted to a Management Group for endorsement. The endorsement of the high level group is considered to be an important aid in obtaining the necessary co-operation for the evaluations.

Independent evaluators also require some mechanism by which results may be communicated and considered as an input to decision-making. Independent evaluations may take several forms. At one end of the scale there are purely academic exercises which, though they are not connected formally to the policy-making system, may still arouse interest and affect decisions. Academics are often involved in methodological development. A second group, consisting mainly of commercial companies, is almost exclusively concerned with quantitative techniques and relies on its mastery of key bibliometric and patent data bases. In keeping with their commercial function, these companies generally work under contract to science administrations. They are also active in the development of these techniques. Finally, there are independent evaluators, typically academics in the field of science policy or consultants, who are commissioned to carry out full-scale evaluations, normally on an *ad hoc* basis and in situations where there is no internal capability or where demonstrated independence is required. These evaluators carry both the advantages and disadvantages of independence. In favour is the chance to draw upon a varied experience and unbiased view of the organisation and against are possible lack of sufficient knowledge about the programme or organisation and a potential confidentiality risk or temptation to self-promotion. Professional ethics for evaluators are important and many problems can be avoided by appropriate interaction and cross-checking with those being evaluated.

C. COST OF EVALUATION

In the search for improved performance and information it would be easy to develop a requirement for an ever increasing amount of evaluation. This is, of course, limited by the cost of evaluation. Cost may be incurred in at least three separate ways:
-   Direct costs of evaluation staff, travel and overheads;
-   Opportunity cost of the time of those involved in peer review; and
-   Cost to the organisation or other object of evaluation in terms of time and disruption.

Direct costs vary but a figure often quoted is one per cent of the programme budget. This figure is formally mandated for the US National Institutes of Health, but in practice has not been reached. Probably the most expensive evaluations are those carried out by commercial contractors. One example was an evaluation carried out for the US National Science Foundation of its Materials Research Laboratory Program. Indeed it was a thorough exercise, but the cost was $5-600 000. To operate its peer review and other evaluation activities, the Commission of the European Communities in its guidelines has requested 10-12 million ECUs for the period 1987-91 out of a total budget of 10 billion ECUs. This figure must take into account a necessarily large travel component. The US Department of Energy estimated that each *ex-post* project evaluation carried out by hearings (see Chapter 5) cost $7 000.

Peer review is not cost free. Firstly there are substantial travel and administrative costs and in some types fees may be paid. However, in the typical project allocation process peers are not paid by the funding body. As individuals they are often motivated by the prestige and influence participation brings them, as well as duty to their field. However, it is their parent institution which is paying their salary and time spent on committees could be seen as time forgone from research. The costing is not as simple though, because peer reviews may often benefit from participation, through meeting other participants and through keeping up with the latest developments in their fields.

Finally, the cost to those being evaluated should be considered. Preparing for an evaluation, *ex-ante* or *ex-post* may well involve a considerable time commitment. On the other hand, in the *ex-ante* phase, the need to formulate a project in a structured manner may well have a beneficial effect upon the subsequent research, while an *ex-post* evaluation may aid dissemination or contribute to future research. Other costs which, though more intangible, may occur are disruptive effects, creation of a feeling of anxiety or uncertainty among staff and creation of a defensive atmosphere. These are really the costs of badly conceived and executed evaluations, not of evaluations *per se.* Again, benefits too may be identified from the process as well as the result of the evaluation, including the experience of discussing their problems and formulating their views. Evaluations can provide an extra channel of communication within an organisation.

If it is possible to generalise about the cost of evaluations, given the range of approaches and contexts, it is that the cost should be proportionate to the scale and importance of the programme. Scale reflects the logistical and statistical demands to be made upon the evaluators and importance reflects the value of the anticipated results of the programme. The two may often be correlated but not always. Programmes of an innovative scientific or technical nature or structure are likely to require an increased level of evaluation compared with routine activities.

V. EVALUATION OF SCIENTIFIC RESEARCH IN UNIVERSITIES

A. INTRODUCTION

In this Chapter, evaluation of research carried out in universities and institutions carrying out research of a similar nature will be addressed, with the exception of certain technological and mission-oriented programmes which may support research in universities (see Chapter 6). Inevitably, an evaluation of university research will feature heavily those organisations which are responsible for financing and implementing policy for university research (research councils), generally through the operation of the peer review system. Also included are procedures instigated by the universities themselves in order to allocate resources and maintain academic standards. It is important to note that much of academic life, including the award of professorial chairs or tenure, is governed by a process of evaluation but these aspects are not covered here.

Section B deals with *ex-ante* evaluation at a high level of aggregation, that of fields and areas of science; Section C examines how, at various levels, resources are allocated to individuals, projects, programmes and institutions; Section D with internal or self-initiated evaluations of university research; and Section E with *ex-post* evaluation of projects and programmes; and Section F considers some of the issues raised.

B. ESTABLISHMENT OF PRIORITIES

A problem which has achieved increasing prominence in Member countries is how to establish priorities between fields of science at a time when the demand for resources exceeds the ability of the nation to supply them. At a national level the budget for science is decided politically while the detailed decisions about projects, decisions which require scientific expertise, are left to the scientific community generally through the operation of the peer review system. It is the process of mediation between the directions and opportunities arising from the conduct of scientific research and the wider economic and social demands upon science which involves an interaction between the political bodies and those responsible for the administration and conduct of science. Often it is new initiatives in areas such as information science or biotechnology which come under scrutiny at this level. The total resource available to science is in part dependent upon its ability to command support for these initiatives. As a general rule, in Member countries, the higher the level of aggregation the more likely it is that the decision will be taken at a political level.

Historical precedents are usually important in determining the allocation between fields but where there is pressure for change in the context of low or zero growth, new activities must replace existing ones and a process of evaluation is required. In the United Kingdom, the

Advisory Board for Research Councils (ABRC), which is responsible for allocating the science budget between five research councils, has attempted to address this problem by introducing a concept it terms the flexibility margin. Research Councils are being obliged to produce corporate plans which include identifiable programmes constituting a defined percentage of the budget in this margin. ABRC will directly compare these programmes and shift resources between councils as a result. While this confronts choice between fields, other than by encouraging best case presentations it offers no solution to the problem.

At a lower level of aggregation, the problem of comparability within broad fields was addressed by the Science Policy Division of the Ministry of Education and Science in the Netherlands by establishing a limited number of *ad hoc* state of the art studies at the level of a discipline (e.g. physics). Committees consisting mainly of academics were expected by the Minister to bring forward proposals for setting priorities in the context of a re-allocative zero sum science budget. In terms of method, these exploratory committees (*Verkennings Commissies* or VCs) all used bibliometric methods to some extent but with specific adaptation to their discipline. Thus the VC in biology used as a measure at group level the productivity of the groups in journals with a high impact factor. The VC in chemical research opted instead for a bibliometric analysis at the national level by measuring the relative contribution of Dutch researchers to the 68 most important journals, rated by impact factor, the list being extended by the committee. The committee combined these data with limited peer reviews. The VC in molecular biology and biochemistry opted for a large citation analysis on three levels of aggregation – institutional, departmental and the research group. It combined these results with specific biochemical indicators. The variety of methodological approaches reflected differences in perceptions of their task by the committees. Through use of different units of analysis, the VC in chemical research made recommendations at the level of sub-field or speciality while that in biology delivered its recommendations at the level of university biology departments. The reports also differed in the response which they elicited, that on chemical research building on a consensus and being regarded as a "blueprint for the future of research" while that on biology was attacked in some quarters.

C.   EVALUATION IN THE SELECTION OF RESEARCH

The most elaborated evaluation procedure is that by which research councils allocate resources to individuals, projects or programmes, which is not surprising since this is their *raison d'être*. This is not to say that all systems are identical. The first dimension in which they vary is in the degree of selectivity and concentration. Put another way, this distinction is between the situation where the researcher has funds at his own discretion or has to compete and undergo a selection process. In most countries a dual support system operates where general university income (from whatever source) is supplemented by grants to cover the incremental cost of research.

1.   General university funding

An example where little selectivity is practised is in Japan. Rather, funding is based on the academic entity known as the Koza, a unit headed by a professor. Koza are categorised according to subject area and other criteria and each receives a financial allocation according to this. These funds cover utilities, small research tools, etc., and are intended to provide a basic freedom of research for individual researchers. The main drawback of this approach is that inactive researchers may be funded. In addition, for priority areas there is a scheme for Grants-in-Aid for scientific research which operates a peer review process based on 1 200 scientists who form a pool from which reviewers are drawn.

2. Focus on the individual

The Canadian Natural Sciences and Engineering Research Council (NSERC), which provides grants for basic and applied research in universities, is an example of a research council approach which is more selective than the Koza scheme but which still focuses on the individual, though in the context of specific scientific proposals. The funding level reflects the quality of the potential research contribution. In the main operating grants scheme applicants are required to produce proposals but there is no commitment by the researcher to pursue that line of inquiry once the funds have been awarded. The other main feature of the scheme is that most applicants (about 75 per cent) receive funding. Adjustments take place in terms of changes in the *level* of funding and in terms of these passing into and out of the system.

3. Inflation in peer ratings of project proposals

Most research council systems consider both the past performance of the applicants and the specific proposals put forward. Although a mission-oriented agency, the National Institutes of Health in the USA fund research in universities on the basis of proposals submitted by investigators in much the same way as research councils. A point of particular interest in this version of the peer review system is that it illustrates the problems of operating a system based solely on judgements of scientific merit when resources are constrained. NIH carries out peer review of grant applications through two sequential levels of review known as the dual review system. Most applications in the public health field enter the system through the Division of Research Grants (DRG) whose function is to assign the proposals to one of over sixty scientific review groups known as study sections, the membership of which is drawn from active researchers in the field. Members individually assign ratings according to their own standards of quality and priority scores are derived. Approved proposal summaries are then passed on to Institutes where Councils may make marginal changes to the priority order on the basis of high or low programme priority. Applications are arranged in order of decreasing priority and the "pay line" or the number of projects which can be funded is then determined by the Congressional appropriation for the programme in question.

It is a fundamental assumption in the NIH peer review system that priority scores represent an absolute standard across fields and study sections. In practice, study section members are reluctant to use the full range of scores because they are concerned that other study sections might rate in a more lenient manner and produce priority scores that are more competitive in subsequent Institutes funding decisions. The inevitable result has been an inflationary pressure on priority scores as members attempt to ensure that proposals in their areas are funded by placing them above the pay line. During the 1970s, there was an attempt to address this problem by *normalizing* scores but this was subsequently abandoned. Figure 2 illustrates graphically the process of grade inflation amongst priority scores and how this stopped during the period of normalization only to recommence upon its abandonment. The problem is that while peers may make merit-based judgements within their fields, once cross-field comparison is engaged there is a strong temptation for them to become advocates for their respective fields.

Figure 2

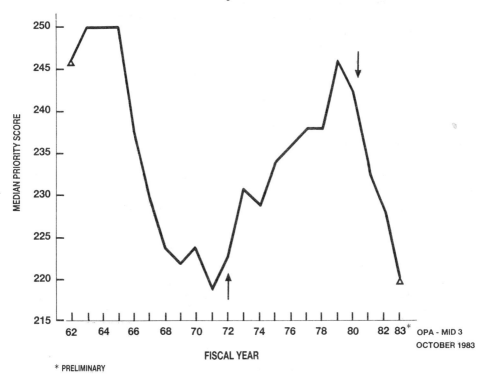

OPA - MID 3
OCTOBER 1983

* PRELIMINARY

4. Provision for termination

An important consideration when policy-makers are trying to devise means to promote a novel research activity is whether to encourage a network approach to link existing research skills or to establish a separate laboratory or institutions. A recurrent problem with the latter option is to decide the length of time selective support is to be applied and how to run down or terminate the activity subsequently. The *Max-Planck-Gesellschaft* (MPG) in Germany operates 50 institutes, each with its own director. Since the late 1960s the term of directors has been altered from life to seven years (renewable) and the society has developed procedures for reviewing performance, the direction of research and the future of each institute.

All Max-Planck institutes have scientific advisory committees which regularly evaluate their research and advise the President of the society. However, these were not considered appropriate for the consideration of long term, more far reaching measures. Instead, several years before the director of an institute or department is due to retire, a special visiting committee appointed by the President and composed of scientific peers with a strong representation from outside Germany makes an extensive survey of the institute's (or department's) recent activity as well as of the overall situation in its research field. Following a site visit and interviews with senior staff, a confidential report is sent to the President advising on whether the institute should be maintained and, if so, whether major changes are necessary in its research profile.

That this process has been effective is demonstrated by an average of one major closure per year for the last twelve years. This has allowed the society to launch several new initiatives with a budget that has remained level in real terms during that period.

5. Institutional evaluation at programme level

The project is not always considered to be the most appropriate unit of operation in *ex-ante* evaluations. In the Federal Republic of Germany the selection of Special Collaborative Research Programmes (*Sonderforschungsbereiche* or SFBs) is an example of programme evaluation where the fitness of a university for an award is considered. This programme was established by the Federal and *Länder* governments following a recommendation by the Science Council (a national advisory body). The object was to create an instrument for promoting specialisation of the universities in research through establishing centres of excellence in science and scholarship. In 1985 there were 162 SFBs at 43 universities costing some DM 300 million. The funds are administered by the *Deutsche Forschungsgemeinschaft* (DFG), a privately organised but publicly funded institution for the promotion of research in all fields. Funds may be provided for up to 15 years on the basis of proposals put forward by individual universities and endorsed by their *Land* government.

The evaluation procedure is conventional in its techniques (two-day site visits at three-year intervals by review committees of peers) but unusual in its scope and effects, and therefore also in the criteria applied. These are evaluations of the universities as institutions and are not confined to the quality of individual proposals or groups. They are explicitly extended to examining the university's quantitative and qualitative assign priority to a certain research field, in terms of its decisions concerning staff and resource allocation, recruitment of personnel (in particular at the professional level) and investments for buildings, libraries, scientific instruments, etc. It is these aspects of long-term development of a university's research profile which justify the considerable formal prerequisites for establishing new SFBs: a positive decision by the DFG requires that the new SFB has been formally endorsed both by the *Land* ministry responsible for its university and by the Science Council.

The review committee, which remains either unchanged or with minor changes over the years, will repeat its evaluation at three-year intervals and thus be able to study the effect of university's effort in its development over time. From the second occasion *ex-ante* evaluation is supplemented by an *ex-post* evaluation, this gives the evaluation the additional benefit of an historical perspective.

Two aspects of this review procedure merit attention. Reviewers are never from a single scientific or scholarly speciality and non-German nationals frequently participate. This is seen as an effective antidote against partisan errors of judgement in a positive or negative sense. The funding decision itself rests upon the review committee's recommendations, but it is taken in a special committee of the DFG with participation of the Federal and *Länder* governments. Scientific members of that committee participate in the site visits, but they do not take part in formulating the reviewers' opinion.

6. Institutional evaluation at the level of national planning

In several countries where universities are reliant on the state for resources there is a tendency towards increasing evaluation but with different approaches and responses. The example referred to in the preceding section represents the only formal evaluation of universities as institutions either in teaching or in research in Germany. It is particularly welcomed by those universities which seek to foster research activities on a par with non-university research institutions. In a situation where there has been no growth in German universities since 1975 they see an imperative to plan for a future in which, with student numbers declining, their overall size, their discipline structure and possibly even their survival as institutions may come to depend more strongly on their research performance.

Another example of evaluation of universities at a national level is the system of *conditional finance*, introduced by the Ministry of Education and Sciences in the Netherlands in 1982. In contrast to the previous liberal system of allocation of block grants to universities, this scheme invited universities to submit research proposals which should include information on the goals of the programme, the reputation of the group, the possible social relevant of the research, the costs and the position of the group within existing networks of national co-ordination. Among the objectives of this reorganisation was the promotion of the cohesion of university research by stimulating groups of researchers to formulate research programmes and to introduce an independent external assessment of these programmes and their results.

The assessment procedure was carried out by evaluation committees in the various disciplines, but these varied in composition and working method, some including international representatives for example. Criteria were imposed by the ministry, being the scientific quality, scientific and social relevance and the size and coherence of the proposals. There was some disquiet that the requirement for programme-type proposals would discriminate against humanities and social sciences which were unused to working at this level of aggregation. The committee's judgement was final and had to be a simple yes or no.

In practice, the criterion of scientific quality was emphasized and that of social relevance often avoided because evaluators regarded it as too controversial. The outcome was that various sciences were dealt with very differently and the institutional relationships between committee members and those evaluated also had effects. As a result, the 1984 procedure has been modified with guidelines expressed more clearly and a formal interaction procedure introduced.

Where the resources in question are for general university funding, not specific projects or programme, the evaluation exercise can acquire an enormous scale and complexity. Such has been the situation in an ongoing exercise carried out by the University Grants Committee (UGC) in the United Kingdom. This body has mediated between the government and the universities and traditionally only made specific funding recommendations at the margins. During the 1980s its role has changed and in a general environment of financial stringency it has been obliged to pass budget cuts on to individual universities with specific suggestions to each as to how it might restructure itself in the light of reduced funds. Also operative in this restructuring is an intention to fund universities more selectively by encouraging strengths and eliminating weaknesses and removing duplication in the system as a whole. There is a belief that funding of university teaching and research ought to be more clearly differentiated with different criteria applying.

It was recognised by the UGC that there was little in the way of systematic data on the performance and standing of the various departments and disciplines in each of the universities. It had little choice but to ask the universities individually to demonstrate, by whatever means they found adequate, where their strengths lay. The initial part of this "planning exercise" was completed in November 1985 and has been used with other data to make specific recommendations. The major methodological problem with this approach has been that each university has developed its own criteria and comparability has been difficult. More objective indicators being used include data on numbers of graduate students, research staff and external grants from research councils and industry. More emphasis is being placed on grants from research councils, implying that the output of their peer review system is being taken as an index of quality. The evaluation measure which has caused most concern among academics concerns the use of publications. Each department was asked to list five publications which were *most representative* of its research output during the preceding five years. No indication was given of the use to which this list would be put. So far, little use has been made of citation methods.

7.   The peer review system

There is little doubt that in most Member countries the peer review system remains the dominant mechanism for *ex-ante* resource allocation. In no case, for example, was bibliometrics regarded as a substitute though most peer reviews consider past publications of applicants as a relevant factor. This illustrates an important point, that while the purpose in project selection is *ex-ante*, any consideration of the ability of the researchers to perform the research must involve an appraisal of their past performance. This may be explicit or rely on the reviewers' general knowledge of the field. In a sense, the more the system is researcher-oriented, as in Japan or Canada, the more reliance is placed upon the judgement of those researchers as to what the scientific priorities should be. In more project-oriented systems, the reviewer is exerting a control over the direction of development of the subject. A positive benefit of the project system is that it is easier to concentrate scarce resources when they are most needed and it obliged the researcher to formulate objectives and workplans in a clear manner. The tension is that too much selectivity excludes sources of new ideas, and unexpected results and too little spreads resources thinly and risks funding inactive researchers.

The exercise becomes altogether more problematic when the level of aggregation is raised. The German case, implying additional resources and focused upon well defined programme proposals has encountered few difficulties. Difficulties however, have arisen in the Dutch and British examples where the scope is extended to most or all of the university system. In the Netherlands, programme proposals were solicited to provide a unit of analysis, but the British case attempts to address the whole system with what must be regarded as a data base of uneven quality together with an inadequate resource base at the centre to process adequately the large volume of information collected.

D.   SELF-INITIATED EVALUATIONS OF UNIVERSITY RESEARCH

1.   External reviews

It is not always the case that evaluations of university research are instigated by funding bodies or government planners external to the university. Evaluations may also be used within the university as a means of maintaining or improving standards. One such approach is the systematic external review carried out, in American and Canadian universities. Typically, departments or programmes are reviewed say every five years by a visiting group of scientific peers. A well articulated scheme is in operation at Rutgers University (US) where the process begins with the selection of a review panel of 2-4 members nominated by professional organisations, funding agencies or major journal editors. The group receives a package of documents centred upon a narrative self-study by the department chairman describing the development of the discipline on campus, its goals and objectives and some statistical information on enrolment as well as a statement of long range plans for the discipline. Curriculum vitae of faculty members are also appended. Panel visits last two days and address a set of standard questions. Prior to departure the panel presents an oral report (the exit interview) to senior academic officers. This is considered particularly important because individuals may be named, an event which happens rarely in the subsequent written reports except in a positive context.

Until the late 1970s, this system had only minor effects at Rutgers, but the University then undertook a more radical self appraisal and re-allocation of its resources. An internal Task Force recommended the establishment of a standing committee to monitor, review and follow up the external review process, meeting each review team and ensuring consistent quality between external reviews and between those and its own ratings of programmes. A particular problem recognised by the Task Force was the tendency for reviewers to put the best possible light on professional colleagues. The Standing Committee issues advisory statements after considering departmental responses and ultimately the Provost makes specific recommendations concerning the programme and establishes a timetable for their implementation. Since 1981, 5 per cent of the total research fund has been re-allocated as a result.

2. Use of indicators

Two (perhaps rather untypical) examples from Sweden illustrate the application of quantitative indicators within academic institutions. In the first, the sub-faculty of Biological and Geological Sciences at Göteborg University has developed "departmental maps" using six indicators of research activity:

- The number of researchers in the department;
- The number of external contracts;
- The number of grants from primary research councils;
- The number of papers produced;
- Maps of international connections (invited professorships, visitors, etc.); and
- The use of non-Swedish external examiners.

The data which was first collected in 1979 is now routinised and forms part of the sub-faculty's resource allocation system. Interestingly, the package is seen as a useful device for the early spotting of departments with difficulties, allowing deans to take quick remedial actions.

The second example, that of the Karolinska Medico-Surgical Institute is unusual in that it has built up an administrative model which facilitates a more rapid re-allocation of resources from areas of low research activity to those of high activity. Among the principles underlying this model are the notions that allocation of resources should be based on agreed indicators of previous research activity compared with similar departments, and that the redistribution of resources should be gradual and long term. The mechanism was that eight activities were measured and given a value and a calculation performed on this basis. Within the Institute, this model is believed to provide a quantitative indicator of quality, and in an institute devoted to excellence in research, the model serves to focus discussion on this issue more efficiently than in the past. To place the exercise in perspective it should be noted that while SKr 5 million have been redistributed, these represent the flexible component in a total budget of some SKr 800 million over a period of 7 years.

3.   Linkage to resource allocation

What is striking about these examples is not that the processes take place but rather that they have been institutionalised to the degree that sufficient confidence is placed on them to result in re-allocations of resources in a negative as well as positive sense. The Rutgers example had been a conventional review but the creation of the Standing Committee, following an exhaustive review by the Task Force, provides a mechanism to standardize and elicit more sharp-edged comments from review committees. Göteborg uses indicators but the Karolinska Institute is a rare example of a mechanical link between indicators and resources. A question which may be posed is whether such a system will reach an equilibrium and cease to be a positive stimulus. Both at Rutgers and Göteborg the actions arising from a review are now regarded as obvious, particularly if a weakness is identified. In this situation additional resources may still be called for in order to remedy the situation.

E.   *EX-POST* EVALUATION OF PROJECTS AND PROGRAMMES

The point has already been made that in the *ex-ante* allocation of funds by research councils, the past performance of applicants is an important factor for consideration. However, this approach is not designed to yield systematic information about the standing or direction of the programmes concerned and it is in the context that *ex-post* evaluation exercises are undertaken.

1.   Systematic *ex-post* project reviews

Two examples of a comprehensive approach to project evaluation are to be found in Sweden and the USA. In the first case, the Swedish National Research Council (NFR) has sought to establish the quality of the projects it funded across its whole portfolio including biology, physics, mathematics, geosciences and chemistry. The evaluations, which span the years 1977-1980, are carried out by teams of experts including foreign scientists, whose views are given considerable weight. Apart from the issue of quality, the team is encouraged to comment on the mode of research management or any deficiencies in terms of resources. Comments are also sought on the general direction of research funded by NFR as input to formulation of priorities. An unusual feature of these evaluations is that reports on the performance of teams and individuals in receipt of grants are publicly available. As such, it is inevitable that the outputs of these evaluations may be used in the wider context of academic staff development. During the last few years, the NFR has been completing its first cycle of subject area investigations. The question which is currently being considered is the wisdom of starting in cycle over again. The benefit is being able to see the extent of change since the first review but the exercise was costly. An evaluation of the evaluation scheme itself, which included the views of those evaluated, concluded that evaluations had generally been conducted in a satisfactory manner and that their recommendations had largely been followed where it was feasible for the Council or the researchers to do so.

In the US National Science Foundation, the institutionalisation of *ex-post* peer review has gone a stage further. Earlier studies by the Foundation had concluded that (in the Chemistry Division) while about 90 per cent of grantees submitted further proposals to NSF and reviewers did evaluate prior work, these reviews yielded ratings which were too few, ambiguous and not valid measures of the quality of prior work. On the basis of a comparison with a citation-based study it was concluded that the quality of prior work had a surprisingly small effect on the award decision. As a result of those findings and in response to congressional pressure, there has been a significant modification of the peer review process. Reviewers of new proposals are now normally requested to provide explicit comments on prior work and on the basis of these comments provide a summary rating. The data for these comments comes from a modified application form with space for a four page summary of the results of complete work. Given the high re-application rate, most awards are thus evaluated.

2. *Ad hoc* programme evaluation

In several countries, from time to time there are *ex-post* evaluations of research programmes carried out either in support of particular policy objectives (increasing quality or re-allocating resources) or to meet more general requirements for evaluation. Some of these studies are primarily methodological in intention as in the United Kingdom where the Advisory Board for Research Councils (ABRC) commissioned citation, co-citation and co-word models in five research fields in order to evaluate the usefulness of these techniques to policy-makers. A two-stage validation process was applied. In the first, experts took part in a series of workshops mainly aimed at comparing results for consistency with the knowledge of scientific experts. The second stage involved policy-makers assessing the practical value of the techniques. As a result of the studies, the ABRC has endorsed citation and co-citation as worthy of further study and commended their use to research councils while cautioning that they should not be used alone and required knowledgeable interpretation. They concluded that the co-word system required further development. ABRC has recently announced an extensive citation analysis of British science using the journal influence method.

In Canada, the Natural Sciences and Engineering Research Council (NSERC) is undertaking an evaluation which addresses its largest activity, the Operating Grants Program (see Section C). Issues addressed include the quality of the research, the impact of the programme and the functioning of the peer review process. In this latter case where for example, selection criteria for grant applications are being examined, the *ex-post* evaluation will address the evaluation decisions carried out earlier in the process. The methodology is primarily survey-based and included both those receiving grants and those rejected. Output is to be assessed by a variant of peer review in which world class researchers in foreign universities with previous personal experience at a Canadian university will be surveyed. To avoid the problem of a biased sample (see Chapter 4), reviewers will be selected by asking foreign organisations such as NSF to identify highly regarded scientists from a list of former Canadian grantees now in US universities. Bibliometric data is given low priority in the study as it is considered to have a potential bias against French language data and areas where the research relates to concerns that are primarily Canadian and the findings are not of widespread international interest.

In contrast, the Australian Research Grants Council is planning to carry out an *ex-post* evaluation of approximately 50 projects which terminated in 1984. The study will focus on bibliometric evaluation (publications, citations and co-citation). Also the Department of Science is currently investigating the use of bibliometric techniques as they apply to the Australian R&D community as part of a wider study on science and technology indicators.

F. ISSUES IN THE EVALUATION OF SCIENTIFIC RESEARCH IN THE UNIVERSITIES

This investigation has revealed that evaluation is taking place throughout the university system in most Member countries and that it takes place at a multiplicity of levels. The tension lies between the mutual evaluations by scientific peers, which are used to shape the direction and maintain the quality of a discipline, and the wider demands made upon evaluation as an instrument for changing structures, determining the allocation of resources and assessing the performance of an area in contributing to mission objectives. Much of the effort of the organisations studied has been focused upon establishing indicators of quality. Bibliometrics, the use of foreign experts, and other indicators and devices all represent ways in which it is sought to demonstrate quality of science to a wider audience which may not be fully convinced by what it sees as the mutual beneficiaries of the peer review system.

Only in isolated examples were indicators used in a mechanical sense for the allocation of resources but where difficult decisions have to be made, their consideration is becoming more common despite often deeply expressed misgivings about their significance. The allocation mechanisms examined seemed to work best where there was a clearly defined question demanding a yes or a no in response to a well defined project or programme proposal. Where whole areas of science or institutions are under appraisal the process appears altogether more political.

Ex-post evaluations are not directly concerned with the allocation of resources. Why then are they undertaken? In the case of the internally initiated university evaluations and to some extent for the research councils there was the incentive of improving performance by a process of self-scrutiny. There was also pressure from outside the research system and in many cases evaluations were intended to satisfy either an explicit or implicit government requirement that the objectives, implementation and outcome of research expenditure be examined.

VI. EVALUATION OF MISSION-ORIENTED RESEARCH

A. INTRODUCTION

Mission-oriented research is interpreted in this Chapter as including three institutional forms:
- Research council programmes with industrial objectives;
- Extramural research sponsored by government mission agencies;
- Intramural research sponsored by government mission agencies.

Each of these is characterised as having objectives which go beyond excellence in science to include relevance to the perceived economic or social need. In effect, further criteria are applied to the evaluation of research. The first two sections are concerned with how these multiple objectives are reconciled within two types of programme while the third makes a brief comparison with evaluation in the context of an alternative institutional framework for pursuing the objectives, the government laboratory.

B. RESEARCH COUNCIL PROGRAMMES WITH INDUSTRIAL OBJECTIVES

Areas of research with technological objectives, particularly engineering, are evaluated according to a different balance of criteria in the countries studied, even when that research is carried out in universities. As Chapter 4 emphasized, one way in which the criterion of utility or applicability is brought to bear is by the placement of industrial scientists or engineers within the decision-making bodies of the peer review system.

An interesting example of how the criteria of quality and utilisation are balanced is to be found in the Netherlands in the Foundation for Technological Sciences (STW), established in 1981 with the aim of stimulating technological research in higher education institutions. "Utilisation" does not necessarily imply that there is an identified user for the research though this is considered desirable. Selection procedures are in three main stages: in the first round, five experts selected for a specific proposal give their written comments on it (without rating it) and counter-comments by the applicants are attached. Subsequently, the package is sent to twelve individuals who act as a "jury" and are asked to rate the proposal on a series of criteria. The board of STW sets the final priority but almost always follows the jury gradings. STW regards speed of decision and a success rate of over 50 per cent as necessary features of the system. A point which has been reiterated in several countries is that utilisation is essential. That is to say it is far preferable when a user/client shows active commitment to and involvement in a project, for instance by financial support.

An *ex-post* evaluation designed to test this point was carried out by the Canadian Natural Sciences and Engineering Research Council. It addressed two schemes designed to transfer research results from university to industry. As participation rates had been low it was possible to obtain good coverage using telephone surveys of academics, forms and university administrators, supplemented by a smaller number of case studies. The major methodological problem encountered was how to establish the criteria for assessing success and failure. These were found to be multi-dimensional concepts open to dispute on the weight to be placed on each dimension. In this evaluation, criteria used included completion rates, whether the projects would have occurred without support and whether results of most projects have been transferred to Canadian industry.

In Sweden, the National Board for Technical Development (STU), which supports applied and mission-oriented basic research in the engineering sciences, regularly makes peer reviews following the same model as the NFR (see Chapter 5). Such evaluations have been concentrated on the special "selected programme areas" where co-ordinated research is financed in five-year programmes. Thirteen have been covered so far. In parallel, a method concentrating on the industrial and societal benefits of research is being developed. This methodology uses a number of different criteria measuring intermediate effects such as industrial contacts with research institutions, career paths of trained researchers, impact of research on education in engineering and international visibility.

If there is a trend to be observed in this type of evaluation it is that relevance and utility are now expected to be demonstrated in some tangible form, preferably one where the user (usually industrial) is prepared to devote resources of time, facilities or money to the research. In all cases, considerable stress was placed upon the need to maintain the quality of the research and not to treat this as a trade-off with utility. Despite this, there were occasional cases where a drop in quality was sustained in order to meet programme objectives, for example where there was a desire to attract new researchers into a priority area.

C. EXTRAMURAL RESEARCH SPONSORED BY GOVERNMENT MISSION AGENCIES

As with the research council programmes, mission agencies sustain multiple objectives but in this case the object is not so much to reorient university R&D as to achieve the mission objectives. Two agencies in the USA demonstrate how *ex-ante* and *ex-post* evaluation can be used when the mission agency is sponsoring fundamental research. Department of Energy's (DoE) Basic Energy Sciences Program (BES) supports a large programme of energy-related basic research. Individual projects are selected on the basis of peer review but the criterion of meeting mission of objectives is broadly defined. The Department developed a particularly rigorous application of *ex-post* peer review in which a random sample of 129 projects was reviewed by 40 panels of scientific peers who initially were asked to rate their own expertise and possible personal relationship with respect to each project. An analysis of project ratings provided by reviewers from different types of institution (industry, universities and DoE laboratories) was judged as showing that these backgrounds did not significantly affect the results of the assessment. Following perusal of a package of relevant information and hearings with principal investigators, panelists were asked to rate projects on a numerical scale across a series of variables and a composite rating of overall project quality. Having completed this individually, the panels then reached a consensus through discussions. An interesting issue addressed during this evaluation was the assessment of whether there was a substantial quality difference between work carried out in the Department's laboratories and universities. No statistically significant difference was found.

1.   *Ex-ante* programme evaluation

The Office of Naval Research (ONR) in the US Department of Defense funds research which is judged relevant to Navy needs. Fifty six per cent of these funds are spent in universities. ONR operates a similar scheme to that of DoE but had also developed an unusual formal procedure for *ex-ante* evaluation at programme level. ONR assigns its research funds to eight internal Navy organisations, called claimants. These claimants receive a budget for two types of programmes. One type, called "core" consists of long term evolutionary funding and accounts for slightly over half of the ONR budget. The remaining funds are allocated to the other type, called "Accelerated Research Initiative" (ARI), consisting of promising research programme in which funding is concentrated for a limited duration (5 years) in order to accelerate progress. All claimants compete against each other to obtain funding for ARI programmes (accounting for about 5-10 per cent of funds annually).

Evaluation of proposed ARIs by the Planning and Assessment Office at ONR Headquarters (known as 102B) begins in mid-autumn and runs to late spring. The total ONR research programme is divided into 15 technical disciplines called sub-elements. A technical expert from ONR (the monitor) presents a status report on his discipline which includes promising research opportunities. Taken with other research and Navy requirements documents, 102B develops a comprehensive list of priorities which is sent to the claimants to provide technical guidance. In late winter, claimants send brief technical descriptions of their proposed ARIs to 102B, panel areas are indentified and reviewers selected. Panels are asked to address research quality, transition potential and Navy relevance. Experts from universities, government and industry are appointed to examine for the first criterion whereas Navy personnel determine the latter two. Panel members meet in mid-spring and following presentations and questions, reviewers individually rate the programme on a structured form which includes a self-estimate of the reviewer's expertise in the area. The Chairman summarises the preliminary ratings and discussion follows in an attempt to reach consensus scores. The similarity to DoE's BES reviews from which it was derived should be noted. The principal difference is the explicit addition of mission relevance experts to the panel.

After all the programmes have been reviewed they are ranked in priority order and comments are recorded. When all panels have met, 102B examines the panel scores and comments for each programme and claimant priorities, then develops a prioritised list of proposed ARIs which is presented to the ONR Corporate Board in late spring for final approval.

2.   Collaborative research

In the United Kingdom, an innovative evaluation approach has been adopted by the Department of Trade and Industry for its Alvey Programme of Advanced Information Technology. This programme has a complex structure with three ministries providing 50 per cent funding for industry and 100 per cent for universities on condition they collaborate within and across these categories to meet the programme goals. The scale and importance of this approach has led the Directorate to commission a "real time" independent evaluation which combines data collection for an *ex-post* evaluation after five years with a continual feedback of evaluation reports on salient issues as they arise during the programme. This "spoils the experiment" but allows the lessons of the evaluation to be applied quickly in the programme and if necessary in any successor programmes. Another feature of this evaluation is that as well as addressing programme strategy, it also covers the structure and organisation of the programme which includes issues such as the workings of collaboration and intellectual property rights. Such "process" issues are less "technology specific" and hence more easily applied in other contexts.

3. Extramural research

From the American examples it appears clear that a mission agency cannot afford to let the criterion of scientific quality go unattended and each provides examples of well-worked peer review systems. That of ONR, like the German special collaborative programmes in Chapter 5, shows that priorities can be handled more systematically if there are clear alternatives to be considered rather than expecting them to emerge in an *ad hoc* manner. The Alvey evaluation is quite different in scope and approach but offers considerable promise as a method to be pursued when the structure as well as the content of science or technology is under consideration. These are both aspects of the same issue as one cannot be pursued without the other.

D. INTRAMURAL RESEARCH SPONSORED BY GOVERNMENT MISSION AGENCIES

The status and performance of government laboratories have been a matter of consideration in several countries. Major *ad hoc* reviews have been undertaken, for example in Canada. As the example of US DoE in the previous section illustrated, comparison of intramural with extramural research is frequently an issue. Quality of science is a prime concern, though it should be noted that laboratories generally have longer term, more mundane, duties to perform. A general problem of government R & D is the determination of the degree to which a programme has benefited its clients since, as results are often free, there may be a tendency to label the R & D as a good thing without considering the nature or extent of its true value to them.

The National Research Council in Canada, the principal research agency of the Federal Government, is interesting in that assessment of performance takes place through two separate mechanisms, Council Review Committees and Program Evaluation. The former is a peer review system in which eminent experts carry out site visits and consider documentary evidence. Committees rarely comment on individuals, considering rather that their function is to flag new areas of science and provide advice on how to cope with diminishing resources. While the review process was considered adequate for the assessment of quality of research it was not perceived to be satisfying the evaluation requirements of the Canadian Treasury Board. In consequence the Program Evaluation Office was established in order to examine the rationale of the programme, its objectives and its effectiveness in meeting them. However, unlike the Review Committees, the evaluation does not follow the divisional structure but rather relates to the activity structure which makes complementarity between the two difficult. Peer review appears more securely institutionalised, perhaps because the Review Committees are composed of outside experts reporting to the Council itself, while Program Evaluation is carried out by NRC employees. More fundamentally, the example illustrates the point made in Chapter 3, that the system can cope far more easily with assessing the quality of results of research than in forming a judgement about their contribution to social or economic goals. There are both structural and methodological reasons for this. The quality issue is intrinsic to science and is addressed without contradicting its social structure.

Relevance is a broader issue and one where the scientific community must interact with business and other communities driven by a different set of values. At a more practical level, the level of methodological development has not yet allowed those responsible for evaluating economic and social returns on research to carry their arguments with authority except in the most application-oriented areas.

Another critical feature of evaluation of intramural research is its relationship to management and career structures. In this respect, procedures can be quite similar to staff assessment in large industrial laboratories. A fairly typical example of evaluation in staff development is provided by the procedures of the National Aerospace Laboratory in Japan which is among the country's largest government research establishments. The principal evaluation approach is the Director-General's hearing in which every researcher reports to the Director-General and other senior figures on progress and problems. This takes place each October, while a similar process each February consists of each Director explaining his Division's research plan for the financial year. Priorities and budgetary allocations are decided on the basis of these hearings. Mechanisms may vary from country to country but the principle of internal review by management is almost ubiquitous.

1. Level of analysis

The question of an appropriate level of analysis was addressed in the context of evaluation in the major French research organisations. Participants at a seminar organised by the Centre de Prospective et d'Evaluation (CPE) and by the CNRS Science, Technology and Society Programme (1983) examined evaluation procedures and sought to analyse how well they were matched to the different scientific, economic and social objectives. The bulk of evaluation work in the organisations tended to be performed by committees of peers or experts and be aimed at assessing individuals and institutions; on the other hand, it was noted that some organisations undertook very little programme evaluation.

An earlier review by CPE had identified diverse interpretations of what was meant by the concept of a programme, ranging from the individual to the national level.

The seminar referred to above considered that the distinction between fundamental and mission-oriented research was inadequate to classify evaluation practices; however the difference in approach between the various organisations is very instructive.

For institutions engaged in fundamental research such as the CNRS, there are a number of scientific evaluation bodies composed of appointed and elected members (National Committee, Specialised Scientific Commissions, etc.). To the bodies concerned with research areas have recently been added interdisciplinary bodies, whose competence extends to proposing the recruitment of researchers and promotions and also the creation, dissolution or alteration of research teams.

Evaluation is by various methods including commissions, investigative reports and encounters between laboratories working in similar areas. Site visits may take place but these are rare in some organisations. Reports tend to rely heavily on the number of scientific publications but also, increasingly, on the spin-off (patents, contributions to international symposia, teaching, etc.).

Organisations carrying out applied research (e.g. INRA, CEA and CNES) tend to rely more heavily on "encounters" (*confrontations*) than reports.

INRA and CEA have systems for constant monitoring of research, INRA keeping a data bank on its research programmes.

For CNES (the Space Agency) mission relevance can be directly assessed because there are external customers and competitors. The situation is more complicated for CEA (the Nuclear Agency) but it has addressed the problem by structuring itself so as to create a domestic market. The Development Agency, OSTORM, which had opted for the CNRS model, recently changed its evaluation procedures and organisation.

E.   ISSUES IN THE EVALUATION OF MISSION-ORIENTED RESEARCH

At first sight the evaluation of mission-oriented research might seem very straightforward, consisting of a binary gate in which fulfilment of the mission, resulting say in a product, is equivalent to success. Even if the research can be so precisely linked (and efforts to do so have rarely been convincing) there is still the matter of successfully innovating the product and obtaining a return on investment (private or social). This crucial stage is dependent on many factors unconnected with the research and, as Chapter 3 emphasized, the whole process is time-dependent and often so lengthy that by the time an evaluation has taken place it is of little more than academic interest. Nevertheless, demonstrating these links remains a target for evaluators and will continue to do so for as long as the case for research is framed in an investment perspective.

In the meantime, both university and agency sponsored programmes have concentrated in their evaluations upon the more attainable goals of user-involvement and the *ex-ante* and *ex-post* stages. For some mission-oriented agencies, the users are within the same agency and there the organisational challenge is to ensure an "internal market" whereby needs are communicated to those performing the R&D. For another category of mission-oriented research, that performing strategic or underpinning research (for example on standards), clients may be numerous but difficult to identify. The clients themselves may find it difficult to place a value upon the research in question from their point of view. Some research on nuclear safety, for example, may not affect reactor design at all but have instead an effect on the climate of opinion and indirectly upon licensing decisions.

With many countries questioning the appropriate role and scale of government sponsored research, a recurring theme for evaluation has been to compare intramural and extramural research. Most commonly, the criterion of comparison has been that of quality of research, with government laboratories sensitive to the suggestion that they do not perform research of comparable quality to that in universities. However, for mission-oriented research, as with scientific research, evaluation is most securely institutionalised where it is dealing with micro-level issues, the individual or the project. Large scale institutional assessment remains a matter for high level inquiries and ultimately political decisions.

VII. INTERNATIONAL PROGRAMMES

International programmes of research may proceed in a number of forms. The simplest of these probably is the bilateral contact involving visits by scientists to each other's countries for varying durations or other exchanges of results. Multilateral programmes may represent an extension of this type of research by an international organisation in pursuit of its objectives or the establishment of shared facilities to reduce costs of large scale experiments. A third type of programme is one where assistance to developing countries is an objective. Each of these produces additional demands and criteria upon the evaluation exercise, not least among which are the logistical problems of carrying out evaluations where at least part of the work is extra-territorial.

A. BILATERAL PROGRAMMES

An example of how a nation may assess and exploit its bilateral activities is provided by the Division of International Programs in the US National Science Foundation. This Division is responsible for the management of around 30 bilateral agreements and has consistently been under pressure to show that programmes, often begun for foreign policy reasons, are of high scientific quality. More recently there have been pressures to ensure that significant benefits accrue to US science from the programmes. The basic approach is the participant survey where, for example, US scientists supported by the Division's programmes, US hosts of foreign scientists under these programmes, and for comparative purposes US scientists engaged in international activities supported by other divisions of NSF were surveyed by post. Another approach was the use of expert panels, which rated projects against the criteria of scientific benefits, establishment of professional relationships and education and training accomplished. Judgements were also made as to whether international involvement or collaboration was necessary.

An innovative approach to evaluation in the Division has been the use of bibliometric techniques to identify which areas in a US/Italy co-operative programme would be advantageous to the US in the sense that they were characterised by unusually high levels of Italian activity, by relevant investigator intersects between collaborative grants in the years 1980-83 and by bibliometric models built on research activity in 6 fields. Two methods were used to identify research areas in the models that appeared to be relevant to grant work. One was to search the models by the names of Italian scientists (or their US collaborators) and the other to search models by subject terms taken from either the title or a descriptive summary of the grant project.

B. MULTILATERAL COLLABORATION – EUROPEAN COMMUNITY PROGRAMMES

As well as being particularly active in the methodological development of evaluation the Commission of the European Communities has, over a number of years, developed an evaluation strategy for the large scale research activity for which it is responsible. For "shared cost actions" which are carried out by national or private laboratories with a substantial Community financial contribution, an *ex-post* peer review is carried out over a period of 6-8 months and covers scientific and technical achievements, economic and social contribution and effectiveness of management as criteria. For "concerted actions", where the Community only bears the co-ordination costs, a much more limited exercise is carried out consisting of "hearings" over a period of three days with a selection of researchers and potential users interviewed by an expert panel.

In a series of test cases several lessons were derived including one that the effective evaluation of a programme's results depends to a large extent on the precise definition of the programme's scientific, technical and socio-economic objectives. The existence of clear programme objectives was seen to have a direct bearing on the credibility of the evaluation exercise since it reduces the need for value judgements from evaluators. The greatest methodological difficulty was encountered in socio-economic impact assessment where problems in the inherent time lag were reinforced by the difficulty of operationalising some Community objectives. Approaches adopted included the presence of users or cost-benefit specialists in the panels and asking the Advisory Committees to submit statements on the R&D impact at national level. Future plans for evaluation were described in Chapter 4.

C. DEVELOPING COUNTRIES

Developing countries face particularly acutely the question of allocating scarce R&D resources to the optimum use. As such, evaluation offers a potentially vital tool but in smaller countries lack of a suitable administrative infrastructure can inhibit its implementation. To address this problem, the Commonwealth Science Council has organised a series of methodological workshops, initially in the Caribbean, with the intention of identifying and implementing appropriate methods. One proposal is an expert system (RESEVAL) which simulates the peer review process and may be applied by an administrator where sufficient expertise is not available.

The Canadian development agency, the International Development Research Corporation (IDRC) is an autonomous public corporation which supports research into the problems of developing countries and helps them build up research capabilities in national institutions. Evaluation is used extensively and it is often carried out by nationals of the developing country concerned, which aims to introduce the perspective of that country and to build an indigenous evaluation capability. The methodological experience of IDRC is that simple approaches are best, as advanced techniques such as economic analysis of rates of return are information intensive but fail to provide decision-makers with guidance for resource allocation decisions. Limited time and resources and the weak data bases encountered in the Third World reinforce this view. Specific methodologies which have been used include survey questionnaires, file analysis, semi-structured interviews, participants observation, citation index searches and cost-benefit analysis.

D. THE INTERNATIONAL "MISSION"

The types of programme described in this section are too disparate to reach clear conclusions which apply to all of them. What they do demonstrate is that international programmes may be seen from a range of perspectives. The US evaluates its activities from the point of view of a participant assessing the benefits of participation while the European Commission acts much as a national administration would to maintain the quality and relevance of its programme. In both cases, key evaluation issues are what research is appropriate for a collaborative rather than national approach and how the benefits of collaboration may be secured. For the developing countries, the message emerging is that evaluation methodologies are not easily transferable to a different context to that in which they were formulated which may have rested upon assumptions of data and human and financial resources which are not available. There is a clear need for appropriate methods to be developed *in situ*.

VIII. CONCLUSIONS

This report set out to explore the "state of the art" in the evaluation of research, at least insofar as this was determinable from the experiences of academics, civil servants and the institutions concerned with this in the Member countries. It was hoped that such a survey would bring to light the different contexts in which research evaluation takes place and indicate the methods and techniques most appropriate or most frequently used in each context. This would allow organisations in Member Countries to assess their own standing in relation to "best practice" across a wide range of types of research activity. Before offering some general features and guidelines which emerged from the data it is worth emphasizing the limitations of this study. First, it was confined to a restricted set of countries and we make no claim that what we have covered applies elsewhere, though we suspect many of the experiences are held in common. Second, within the countries studied, only a limited range of organisations were covered and these were not necessarily the exact equivalents from one country to another. Third, it was not possible to follow up each evaluation covered and to assess its impact on policy-making. The intention was to highlight individual cases of interest and to discern how the scope, purpose, criteria and methods were applied. Fourth, our coverage of mission-oriented research has been of a more limited nature than that of university research and we did not have enough data about private sector practices. What remains, we believe, is an extensive collection of experiences and lessons to be derived from them which will meet the objective of allowing Member countries to appraise their own efforts in comparison with others. A fuller synthesis should be delayed until evaluation has reached a more mature state of development.

The lack of maturity in the development of evaluation is demonstrated by the ambiguousness of the terms in which it is understood. Definitions of evaluation range from strict economic appraisals approaching the question of "value", through systems for allocating resources, to the broad activity of policy-making, monitoring and implementation of policy. Evaluation in this last context can often mean little more than a general review of a subject area. There is also an understanding of evaluation as being equivalent to the application of a single technique, such as citation analysis, to a specific sub-field of science over a prescribed time interval. Between the general review and the highly specific study, there lies a vast middle ground on which individuals, groups and organisations are carrying out, often in an experimental way, evaluations of research of various kinds.

A recurrent problem on this middle ground is the difficulty of specifying adequately beforehand the four interrelated elements – scope, purpose, criteria and organisation of evaluation. One reason for this lies in the institutional complexity in which contemporary scientific research is carried out. Because the various levels of the research system are interdependent, it is often difficult to draw a line round a particular sub-system that needs to be evaluated; or to be confident that the boundary will be respected not only during but after the evaluation. If the boundary between what is internal and what is external to an evaluation is perceived to be constantly changing, the suspicion will be engendered that the results of the evaluation may be used in contexts different from, and for purposes beyond those formerly expressed in the terms of reference. This uncertainty, in turn, can politicise the evaluation perhaps even to the extent of casting doubt on the impartiality of the data gathered and the recommendations made. While it can be readily agreed that each evaluation remains connected in various ways to different parts of the national research system, the interconnection ought to be made more, rather than less, explicit. The point we make is that better evaluations will result if scope, purpose, criteria and mode of organisation are clarified beforehand (see Chapter 2).

In the Introduction it has been suggested that the current upsurge of interest in evaluation owes more to the nature of contemporary science than to the fact that growth rates of the budgets for research have slowed, and in some cases, became negative. The rapid growth of scientific and technological activities during the last 50 years have intensified the spirit of competition within science with the result that research evaluation which has always been implicit to science has become at the same time more explicit and politicised. It is the scientists themselves and their institutional leaders who encourage evaluation because they believe that only in this way will the new most promising areas of science be funded while the others, perhaps with longer histories, will clearly be seen to have had their day. The dynamic nature of science, then, implies that new activities will eventually come to replace older ones and this comes about primarily through the process of creating new specialities. It is the constant, and some would say accelerating, creation of new specialities which sets the key intellectual problems for evaluators; the development of techniques which are capable of making judgements between and across specialities.

If there is a common concern in all the evaluations we have encountered, it is that of judging the value or the quality of one area of science against another. It is a problem partly because those who currently command centre stage in cognitive or institutional terms do not want to abandon their position but it is also a problem of the incompatibility, or the incommensurability, of one speciality with another. Each specialisation is specialist because it has established its own research questions and methods as well as its own journals and intellectual leaders. There are currently no techniques available which allow different specialities to be compared and then ranked one with another, though it is important to keep in mind that this sort of comparison and ranking is carried out all the time in the various committees that are responsible for the funding of research. Nonetheless, the rational basis of this decision-making is far from clear. It is perhaps worth noting that while direct comparisons between fields are not possible on cognitive grounds it is possible, by assuming that new fields are likely to be more vital and hold the greatest promise for significant advance to rank new specialities simply by their relative ages. Certain bibliometric techniques are now available which make it a relatively straightforward task to identify new specialities and their intellectual leaders. From this development comes the observation that given the intrinsic difficulties associated with making judgements across specialities, funding agencies may find it easier to rank specialities in terms of age and promote the development of science by supporting youth instead of maturity. Given the speed with which new specialities emerge and their relatively small size, evaluations using these techniques will have the effect of identifying promising individuals more than promising areas in science and it is arguable that since this is what the peer review process is intended to do anyway these bibliometric techniques will give valuable support to a process that is currently under some public scrutiny.

As we have indicated in the earlier chapters peer review is the central method on which most evaluations are based. It operates at all levels of evaluation, over all types of research activity in every national research system. Equally, there is little doubt that peer review is believed to work reasonably well, though there are justifiable criticisms about its appropriateness in particular instances. Some of these are given in Chapter 3 and we do not propose to repeat them here. We simply wish, in these concluding remarks, to underline the fact that many countries are experimenting with peer review; trying to find forms which are more able to cope with the complexities of contemporary science. There experiments have taken two specific forms; broadening the base of expertise; and introducing new forms of information to the decision-making process of which that provided by bibliometric analysis of various kinds is currently predominant but not necessarily the most significant. It is perhaps worth stressing that even though bibliometric methods are diffusing into the peer review process it has been slow and, in no case, have we found substantial support for the idea that these methods will eventually replace peer review. Much more significant, we feel, is the growing use of social science methods – that is questionnaires and structured interviews of various kinds – to gather evaluative information about individuals, programmes and institutions. To the extent that this is well done and the results interpreted with subtlety, there are coming into existence information networks which could directly challenge the authority of peer review committees. Surveys can reach a larger number of practising scientists on virtually any issue, whereas peer review is by its nature, a judgement by the few over the many. What would happen, then, if the respective evaluations did not agree? Could such an event overturn the decisions of the peer review process? Could the panel of peers respond by carrying out a survey of its own? Given the speed with which new specialities emerge in science and given the steady drift in science away from paper to electronic forms of communications, is it unreasonable to forecast that peer review itself will be broadened to include virtually all of the relevant community, whose opinions will be gathered electronically and whose judgements will be administered by a scientifically literate, but not specialist, bureaucracy?

Peer review can, of course, be broadened in various ways. Among the most challenging, currently, is to use expert consensus as the vehicle for evaluating programmes, scientific facilities, and institutions which have clearly defined socio-economic objectives. Without rehearsing here the various attempts that have been made in Member countries to deal with the question of whether the research carried out did or did not contribute to broader socio-economic objectives, it is worth drawing attention to the tendency, in these situations, to separate the scientific and the non-scientific aspects of the decision-making process. Here, a *modus operandi* can be established by first of all passing the research through a standard peer review aimed at determining its scientific quality and subsequently, handing on the "best science" to a higher level committee to decide which science is useful in relation to objectives. This *modus operandi* has grown up in part because it provided a first line of defence for mission-oriented agencies against the charge that in striving to attain their objectives they are using inferior science. It is worth noting that while this way of operating is useful when evaluation is carried out *ex-ante*, it does not deal at all with the extent to which the research did or did not contribute to mission objectives; that is with *ex-post* evaluations.

It is in the context of *ex-post* evaluation that the question is increasingly being asked whether one is getting "value for money" from investments in scientific research. In both the elaboration of methods of evaluation and in the experiences of evaluation practices of Member countries, the development of value for money criteria lags considerably behind other criteria aimed at determining the quality of scientific activity. The principal reason for this is not hard to find: the processes that link scientific discovery to economic growth are complex and, often, indirect. In particular, the relationships of scientific research to technological innovation do not lend themselves easily to cost benefit analyses. Usually, if one wants to gain an understanding of the ways in which scientific knowledge enters the innovation process one must be content to use the techniques that are more common to the historian than to the economist but, even here, scholars have found it difficult to generalise the knowledge gained from detailed case studies into value for money criteria. There is much research needed here and this is recognised most clearly by those who would be consumers of a genuine economics of research. As one member of Congress in the USA has expressed that "the time has passed when the economic value of certain lines of research can be justified by anecdote, yet short of full scale case studies of major innovations there is little offered in the way of guidance from current techniques and methods".

If the techniques and methods of evaluation are still in a relatively undeveloped state, one reason for this might be the apparent lack of interaction of evaluation with the relevant decision-making processes. There is much evidence from the country studies that such evaluations as do occur are not systematically related to subsequent resource allocation processes. Evaluation reports, it is true, are often said to act as inputs to future decision-making, but as far as we have been able to determine their impact is at best indirect. Arguably, this is because there is a very important link in the decision-making process between *ex-ante* and *ex-post* evaluations which really should be forged more strongly. *Ex-ante* evaluations are still largely the preserve of one of the many varieties of expert consensus while *ex-post* evaluations are increasingly becoming the preserve of a cadre of professional evaluators. Unless great care is taken, this situation will set the stage for a breakdown of communication between the one and the other. Yet, *ex-ante* evaluation in the end requires the information held by the expert evaluator if the next generation of programmes is to build in a coherent way upon previous investments. This is all the more important when research is being planned over a very long time horizon and where broader considerations than purely scientific merit are involved. It would, we think, be a mistake to cultivate an ethos of evaluation where the separation of expert consensus and professional evaluations was virtually assured.

The interviews we have carried out and the data we have been able to gather in this study can only provide a snapshot of the state of art of evaluation in member countries. If one thing is indisputable, it is that evaluations of research are becoming more central in the formulation of national research policy and for this reason it will be necessary to continue to collect data on national experiences with evaluations of various kinds. There is also a need to extend the present work to consider more adequately the implications for the social sciences and the humanities of current trends in the methods and techniques for evaluation being developed. There is currently widespread concern that techniques developed out of models based on performance in the natural sciences may be extended uncritically to the social sciences and humanities as well.

It will also be important to look more closely than we have been able to at the evaluation practices of mission-oriented agencies of the Member countries. The question of the contribution that research makes to national social and economic performance is perennial in science policy and much value could be gained from a more detailed survey of methods and practices in those areas where quality of research is only one of the objectives to be obtained.

From our research we have concluded that the evaluation of research, even basic research, is often carried out independently of the institutional structures, forms of organisation and management practices that provide the infrastructure of scientific research. Since it is unlikely that excellence in science is independent of the concrete context in which it takes place or, as often seems to be said, that it depends solely on the presence or otherwise of funding, there is a good case for evaluating the structures that are supposed to deliver scientific knowledge and for the careful analysis of the effects of evaluation on subsequent research performance.

NOTES AND REFERENCES

1. Workshop on Science and Technology Indicators in the Higher Education Sector, OECD, Paris, 10-13 June 1985.
2. Report of the Workshop on the Evaluation of the Effectiveness of Government Measures for the Stimulation of Innovation, OECD, Paris, 6-7 June 1983, p. 26.

BIBLIOGRAPHY

BARBARIE, A., "Evaluating Government R&D: Beyond 'Quality of Research'", *Performance and Credibility: Developing Excellence in Public and Non-profit Organisations*, ABRAMSON, A., BELLAVITA, C., and WHOLEY, J.S. (Eds.), Lexington Books, Ottawa, pp. 109-116, 1986.

Beraterkommission für die öffentlich geförderte Grossforschung auf dem Gebiet der Biotechnologie: Bericht an das Bundesministerium für Forschung und Technologie, Bonn, 1983.

Bericht der Beraterkommission für das Deutsche Krebsforschungszentrum/Advisory commission for the Deutsches Krebsforschungszentrum, Bonn, 1982.

Bunderministerium für Forschung und Technologie (Ed.): Die Entwicklung der Datenverarbeitung in der Bundesrepublik Deutschland – Programmbewertung der DV-Förderung des BMFT 1967 bis 1979, Bonn, 1982.

COLE, S. and COLE, J.R., "Scientific Output and Recognition: A Study in the Operation of the Reward System in Science", *American Sociological Review*, No. 32, pp. 377-390, 1967.

COLE, S., COLE, J.R. and SIMON, G.A., "Chance and Consensus in Peer Review", *Science*, No. 214, pp. 881-885, 1981.

CPE Etude No. 51, Colloque international CPE, "Méthodologies évaluatives de la recherche, vol. 2: les programmes de recherche", Centre de Prospective et d'Evaluation, Paris, 1985.

CPE Etudes 29.1 and 29.2, "L'évaluation des programmes de recherche scientifique; rapport du séminaire sur l'évaluation des programmes dans les grands organismes français de recherche", Centre de Prospective et d'Evaluation, Paris, 1983.

Deutsche Forschungsgemeinschaft (Ed.): Sonderforschungsbereiche, Grundlagen des Förderungsprogramms und Verfahrensregeln, Bonn, 1983.

DU BUISSON, C., "Experience with Auditing French Research Organisations", contribution to the Meeting of the "Six Countries Programme", Windsor (UK), November 1982.

FREEMAN, C., "Recent Developments in Science and Technology Indicators – A Review", SPRU, University of Sussex, UK, 1982.

GIBBONS, M., "Methods for the Evaluation of Research", *International Journal of Institutional Management in Higher Education,* vol. 9, No. 1, pp. 79-85, March 1985.

HEERINGEN, A. van, "Cluster-Analysis of the Publication-Output of Fundamental Research in Exact and Natural Sciences", paper presented at the OECD Workshop on Science and Technology Indicators in the Higher Education Sector, OECD, Paris, 10-13 June 1985.

IRVINE, J. and MARTIN, B.R., "What Direction for Basic Scientific Research?", *Science and Technology Policy in the 1980s and Beyond*, GIBBONS, M., GUMMETT, P. and UDGANKAR, B. M. (Eds.), Harlow, Longman, pp. 67-98, 1984.

KREILKAMP, K., "Hindsight and the Real World of Science Policy", *Science Studies*, vol. 1, No. 1, p. 43, 1971.

MACAULEY, J.B., "An Indicator of Excellence in Canadian Science", Statistics Canada, April 1985.

MARTIN, B.R. and IRVINE, J., "Output Indicators for Science Policy: An Evaluation of CERN's Past Performance: And Future Prospects", paper presented at the OECD Workshop on Science and Technology Indicators in the Higher Education Sector, OECD, Paris, 10-13 June 1985.

Max-Planck-Gesellschaft (Ed.): *Jahrbuch 1984*, Göttingen, 1984.

METCALFE, J.S. and GEORGHIOU, L.G., "An Investment Framework for Science", Report to UK Advisory Board for Research Councils, September 1985.

MEYER-KRAHMER, F., "Recent Results in Measuring Innovation Output", paper presented at the OECD Workshop on Patent and Innovation Statistics, OECD, Paris, June 1982.

Mitre Corporation, "Evaluative Study of the Materials Research Laboratory Program", MTR 7764, September 1978.

MOED, H.F., BURGER, W.J.M., FRANKFORT, J.G. and Van RAAN, A.F.J., "On the Measurement of Research Performance: The Use of Bibliometric Indicators", Research Policy Unit, Diensten OWZ/PISA, State University of Leiden, Leiden, The Netherlands, 1983.

MOED, H.F., BURGER, W.J.M., FRANKFORT, J.G. and Van RAAN, A.F.J., "The Use of Bibliometric Data for the Measurement of University Research Performance", *Research Policy*, No. 14, pp. 131-149, 1985.

MORAVCSIK, M.J., "The Assessment of Scientific Output", paper presented at the OECD Workshop on Science and Technology Indicators in the Higher Education Sector, OECD, Paris, 10-13 June 1985.

NARIN, F. and GEE, H.H., "An Analysis of Research Publications Supported by NIH 1970-1976", NIH Program Evaluation Report, US Department of Health and Human Services, December 1980.

NARIN, F., "Measuring the Research Productivity of Higher Education Institutions using Bibliometric Techniques", paper presented at the OECD Workshop on Science and Technology Indicators in the Higher Education Sector, OECD, Paris, 10-13 June 1985.

NARIN, F., *Evaluative Bibliometrics: The Use of Publication and Citation Analysis in the Evaluation of Scientific Activity*, NSF, Washington D.C., 1976.

National Science Board, *Science Indicators*, US Government Printing Office, Washington D.C.

National Science Foundation, "Fairness of the NSF Award Decision Process – Fiscal Year 1982", Evaluation Staff Study, NSF, Washington D.C., 1982.

National Science Foundation, "Fairness of the NSF Award Decision Process – Fiscal Year 1983", Evaluation Staff Study, NSF, Washington D.C., 1983.

National Science Foundation, "Study of Patents Resulting from NSF Chemistry Program", Research Corporation Invention Administration Program, NSF, Washington D.C., September 1982.

OECD Report of the Workshop on the Evaluation of the Effectiveness of Government Measures for the Stimulation of Innovation, OECD, Paris, 6-7 June 1983.

OECD Science and Technology Indicators Conference, OECD, Paris, 1980.

Office of the Comptroller General, *Evaluating Research and Experimental Development Programs*, Ottawa, (exposure draft, December 1984, final forthcoming).

Office of the Comptroller General, *Guide on the Program Evaluation Function*, Ottawa, 1981.

Office of the Comptroller General, *Principles for the Evaluation of Programs*, Ottawa, 1981.

PAVITT, K.L.R., "R&D Patenting and Innovative Activities: A Statistical Exploration", *Research Policy*, vol. 1, No. 2, pp. 33-51, 1982.

PINSKI, G. and NARIN, F., "Citation Influence for Journal Aggregates of Scientific Publications: Theory, with Application to the Literature of Physics", *Information Processing and Management*, vol. 12, No. 5, pp. 297-312, 1976.

ROTHMAN, H., "ABRC Science Policy Study: Further Studies on the Evaluation and Measurement of Scientific Research", Report for UK Economic and Social Research Council, August 1985.

SAVIOTTI, P.P. and METCALFE, J.S., "Technological Output Indicators, Product Characteristics and Industrial Performance", paper presented at the OECD Workshop on Patent and Innovation Statistics, OECD, Paris, June 1982.

SCHNEIDER, Ch., "A programme for collaborative research in universities", Europe Science Foundation, (Ed.): *Proceedings of the ESRC/NSF Symposium, "Rise and Fall of a Priority Field"*, Strasbourg, 1986.

SMALL, H., and SWEENEY, E., "Clustering the Science Citation Index Using Co-citations, I. Comparison of Methods", *Scientometrics 7* (3-6), pp. 391-409, 1985.

STACKMANN, K. and STREITER, A. (Eds.): Sonderforschungsbereiche 1969-1984. Bericht über ein Förderungsprogramm der Deutschen Forschungsgemeinschaft, Weinheim, 1985.

Status und Perspektiven der Grossforschungseinrichtungen. Bericht der Bundersregierung (Bundestagsdrucksache 10/1327), Bonn, 1984.

TURNER, W., CHARTRON, G. and MICHELET, B., "Describing Scientific and Technological Problem Networks using Manually and Automatically Indexed Full Text Data Bases: Some Co-word Analysis Techniques", paper presented at the OECD Workshop on Science and Technology Indicators in the Higher Education Sector, OECD, Paris, 10-13 June 1985.

Westdeutsche Rektorenkonferenz (Ed.), Effizienz der Hochschulen. WRK-Kolloquium 1./2.10.1979, Bonn, 1980 (Dokumente zur Hochschulreform XXXVII, 1980).

WHITE, H.D. and GRIFFITH, B.C., "Author Co-citation: a Literature Measure of Intellectual Structure", *JASIS 32* (3), pp. 162-171, 1981.

Wissenschaftsrat (1981): Stellungnahmen zu geisteswissenschaftlichen Forschungseinrichtungen ausserhalb der Hochschulen, Köln, 1981.

Wissenschaftsrat (1982): Stellungnahmen zu den Wirtschaftsforchungsinstituten und zum Forschungsinstitut für Rationalisierung, Köln, 1982.

Wissenschaftsrat (1984): Stellungnahme zu erziehungswissenschaftlichen Einrichtungen ausserhalb der Hochschulen, Köln, 1984.

LIST OF PARTICIPANTS IN THE *AD HOC* GROUP ON SCIENTIFIC AND UNIVERSITY RESEARCH

at its Meeting of 16th June 1986

Chairman: Mr. V. von Massow, Germany

Mr. G. McAlpine
Australia

Mr. G. Julien
Canada

Mr. M. Korst
Denmark

Mr. P. Montigny
France

Mr. J. Schlegel
Germany

Mr. A. Akritopoulos
Greece

Mrs. S. Avveduto Soldatini
Italy

Mr. M. Ikari
Japan

Mr. H. Endo
Japan

Mr. J. van Haastrecht
Netherlands

Mr. C. Navarro
Spain

Mr. A. Bennassar
Spain

Mr. J. Baumann
Switzerland

Mr. P. Wollants
Belgium

Mr. J.R. de la Mothe
Canada

Mrs. H. Kuusi
Finland

Miss A. Rouban
France

Mr. G. Christou
Greece

Mr. A. Matteucci
Italy

Mr. A. Ichikawa
Japan

Mr. S. Nakao
Japan

Mr. P. Fenger
Netherlands

Mr. T. Sirevag
Norway

Mr. A. Cadenas
Spain

Mrs. K. Eliasson
Sweden

Mr. M.F. Hipkins
United Kingdom

Mr. R. Piekarz
United States

Mr. F. Romano
EEC

Miss E. Spachis
EEC

Secretariat

Mr. J.D. Bell
Mrs. M. Solanes
Mr. G. Drilhon
Mr. P. Levasseur
Mr. L. Georghiou (Consultant)
Mr. M. Gibbons (Consultant)

OECD SALES AGENTS
DÉPOSITAIRES DES PUBLICATIONS DE L'OCDE

ARGENTINA - ARGENTINE
Carlos Hirsch S.R.L.,
Florida 165, 4º Piso,
(Galeria Guemes) 1333 Buenos Aires
Tel. 33.1787.2391 y 30.7122

AUSTRALIA-AUSTRALIE
D.A. Book (Aust.) Pty. Ltd.
11-13 Station Street (P.O. Box 163)
Mitcham, Vic. 3132 Tel. (03) 873 4411

AUSTRIA - AUTRICHE
OECD Publications and Information Centre,
4 Simrockstrasse,
5300 Bonn (Germany) Tel. (0228) 21.60.45
Local Agent:
Gerold & Co., Graben 31, Wien 1 Tel. 52.22.35

BELGIUM - BELGIQUE
Jean de Lannoy, Service Publications OCDE,
avenue du Roi 202
B-1060 Bruxelles Tel. (02) 538.51.69

CANADA
Renouf Publishing Company Ltd/
Éditions Renouf Ltée,
1294 Algoma Road, Ottawa, Ont. K1B 3W8
Tel. (613) 741-4333
Toll Free/Sans Frais:
Ontario, Quebec, Maritimes:
1-800-267-1805
Western Canada, Newfoundland:
1-800-267-1826
Stores/Magasins:
61 rue Sparks St., Ottawa, Ont. K1P 5A6
Tel: (613) 238-8985
211 rue Yonge St., Toronto, Ont. M5B 1M4
Tel: (416) 363-3171
Sales Office/Bureau des Ventes:
7575 Trans Canada Hwy, Suite 305,
St. Laurent, Quebec H4T 1V6
Tel: (514) 335-9274

DENMARK - DANEMARK
Munksgaard Export and Subscription Service
35, Nørre Søgade, DK-1370 København K
Tel. +45.1.12.85.70

FINLAND - FINLANDE
Akateeminen Kirjakauppa,
Keskuskatu 1, 00100 Helsinki 10 Tel. 0.12141

FRANCE
OCDE/OECD
Mail Orders/Commandes par correspondance :
2, rue André-Pascal,
75775 Paris Cedex 16
Tel. (1) 45.24.82.00
Bookshop/Librairie : 33, rue Octave-Feuillet
75016 Paris
Tel. (1) 45.24.81.67 or/ou (1) 45.24.81.81
Principal correspondant :
Librairie de l'Université,
12a, rue Nazareth,
13602 Aix-en-Provence Tel. 42.26.18.08

GERMANY - ALLEMAGNE
OECD Publications and Information Centre,
4 Simrockstrasse,
5300 Bonn Tel. (0228) 21.60.45

GREECE - GRÈCE
Librairie Kauffmann,
28, rue du Stade, 105 64 Athens Tel. 322.21.60

HONG KONG
Government Information Services,
Publications (Sales) Office,
Beaconsfield House, 4/F.,
Queen's Road Central

ICELAND - ISLANDE
Snæbjörn Jónsson & Co., h.f.,
Hafnarstræti 4 & 9,
P.O.B. 1131 – Reykjavik
Tel. 13133/14281/11936

INDIA - INDE
Oxford Book and Stationery Co.,
Scindia House, New Delhi 1 Tel. 331.5896/5308
17 Park St., Calcutta 700016 Tel. 240832

INDONESIA - INDONÉSIE
Pdii-Lipi, P.O. Box 3065/JKT.Jakarta
Tel. 583467

IRELAND - IRLANDE
TDC Publishers - Library Suppliers,
12 North Frederick Street, Dublin 1.
Tel. 744835-749677

ITALY - ITALIE
Libreria Commissionaria Sansoni,
Via Lamarmora 45, 50121 Firenze
Tel. 579751/584468
Via Bartolini 29, 20155 Milano Tel. 365083
Sub-depositari:
Editrice e Libreria Herder,
Piazza Montecitorio 120, 00186 Roma
Tel. 6794628
Libreria Hœpli,
Via Hœpli 5, 20121 Milano Tel. 865446
Libreria Scientifica
Dott. Lucio de Biasio "Aeiou"
Via Meravigli 16, 20123 Milano Tel. 807679
Libreria Lattes,
Via Garibaldi 3, 10122 Torino Tel. 519274
La diffusione delle edizioni OCSE è inoltre
assicurata dalle migliori librerie nelle città più
importanti.

JAPAN - JAPON
OECD Publications and Information Centre,
Landic Akasaka Bldg., 2-3-4 Akasaka,
Minato-ku, Tokyo 107 Tel. 586.2016

KOREA - CORÉE
Kyobo Book Centre Co. Ltd.
P.O.Box: Kwang Hwa Moon 1658,
Seoul Tel. (REP) 730.78.91

LEBANON - LIBAN
Documenta Scientifica/Redico,
Edison Building, Bliss St.,
P.O.B. 5641, Beirut Tel. 354429-344425

MALAYSIA - MALAISIE
University of Malaya Co-operative Bookshop
Ltd.,
P.O.Box 1127, Jalan Pantai Baru,
Kuala Lumpur Tel. 577701/577072

NETHERLANDS - PAYS-BAS
Staatsuitgeverij
Chr. Plantijnstraat, 2 Postbus 20014
2500 EA S-Gravenhage Tel. 070-789911
Voor bestellingen: Tel. 070-789880

NEW ZEALAND - NOUVELLE-ZÉLANDE
Government Printing Office Bookshops:
Auckland: Retail Bookshop, 25 Rutland Street,
Mail Orders, 85 Beach Road
Private Bag C.P.O.
Hamilton: Retail: Ward Street,
Mail Orders, P.O. Box 857
Wellington: Retail, Mulgrave Street, (Head
Office)
Cubacade World Trade Centre,
Mail Orders, Private Bag
Christchurch: Retail, 159 Hereford Street,
Mail Orders, Private Bag
Dunedin: Retail, Princes Street,
Mail Orders, P.O. Box 1104

NORWAY - NORVÈGE
Tanum-Karl Johan
Karl Johans gate 43, Oslo 1
PB 1177 Sentrum, 0107 Oslo 1 Tel. (02) 42.93.10

PAKISTAN
Mirza Book Agency
65 Shahrah Quaid-E-Azam, Lahore 3 Tel. 66839

PORTUGAL
Livraria Portugal,
Rua do Carmo 70-74, 1117 Lisboa Codex.
Tel. 360582/3

SINGAPORE - SINGAPOUR
Information Publications Pte Ltd
Pei-Fu Industrial Building,
24 New Industrial Road No. 02-06
Singapore 1953 Tel. 2831786, 2831798

SPAIN - ESPAGNE
Mundi-Prensa Libros, S.A.,
Castelló 37, Apartado 1223, Madrid-28001
Tel. 431.33.99
Libreria Bosch, Ronda Universidad 11,
Barcelona 7 Tel. 317.53.08/317.53.58

SWEDEN - SUÈDE
AB CE Fritzes Kungl. Hovbokhandel,
Box 16356, S 103 27 STH,
Regeringsgatan 12,
DS Stockholm Tel. (08) 23.89.00
Subscription Agency/Abonnements:
Wennergren-Williams AB,
Box 30004, S104 25 Stockholm.
Tel. (08)54.12.00

SWITZERLAND - SUISSE
OECD Publications and Information Centre,
4 Simrockstrasse,
5300 Bonn (Germany) Tel. (0228) 21.60.45
Local Agent:
Librairie Payot,
6 rue Grenus, 1211 Genève 11
Tel. (022) 31.89.50

TAIWAN - FORMOSE
Good Faith Worldwide Int'l Co., Ltd.
9th floor, No. 118, Sec.2
Chung Hsiao E. Road
Taipei Tel. 391.7396/391.7397

THAILAND - THAILANDE
Suksit Siam Co., Ltd.,
1715 Rama IV Rd.,
Samyam Bangkok 5 Tel. 2511630

TURKEY - TURQUIE
Kültur Yayinlari Is-Türk Ltd. Sti.
Atatürk Bulvari No: 191/Kat. 21
Kavaklidere/Ankara Tel. 25.07.60
Dolmabahce Cad. No: 29
Besiktas/Istanbul Tel. 160.71.88

UNITED KINGDOM - ROYAUME-UNI
H.M. Stationery Office,
Postal orders only:
P.O.B. 276, London SW8 5DT
Telephone orders: (01) 622.3316, or
Personal callers:
49 High Holborn, London WC1V 6HB
Branches at: Belfast, Birmingham,
Bristol, Edinburgh, Manchester

UNITED STATES - ÉTATS-UNIS
OECD Publications and Information Centre,
2001 L Street, N.W., Suite 700,
Washington, D.C. 20036 - 4095
Tel. (202) 785.6323

VENEZUELA
Libreria del Este,
Avda F. Miranda 52, Aptdo. 60337,
Edificio Galipan, Caracas 106
Tel. 32.23.01/33.26.04/31.58.38

YUGOSLAVIA - YOUGOSLAVIE
Jugoslovenska Knjiga, Knez Mihajlova 2,
P.O.B. 36, Beograd Tel. 621.992

Orders and inquiries from countries where Sales
Agents have not yet been appointed should be sent
to:
OECD, Publications Service, Sales and
Distribution Division, 2, rue André-Pascal, 75775
PARIS CEDEX 16.

Les commandes provenant de pays où l'OCDE n'a
pas encore désigné de dépositaire peuvent être
adressées à :
OCDE, Service des Publications. Division des
Ventes et Distribution. 2. rue André-Pascal. 75775
PARIS CEDEX 16.

70712-04-1987

UNITED KINGDOM - ROYAUME-UNI
(01)211-5656

OECD PUBLICATIONS, 2, rue André-Pascal, 75775 PARIS CEDEX 16 - No. 44027 1987
PRINTED IN FRANCE
(92 87 05 1) ISBN 92-64-12981-2